"Tara Well is an extraordinarily creative ṛ
she introduces a powerful new approach
people to look at themselves and each other with compassion and clarity.
As our world becomes more complex and uncertain, there's an urgent need
for this book. *Mirror Meditation* is a truly unique offering that is sure to
change the lives of many readers worldwide and how they literally see
themselves."

—**Scott Barry Kaufman, PhD**, host of *The Psychology Podcast*,
and author of nine books, including *Transcend*

"*Mirror Meditation* is an important contribution to understanding how we
see ourselves and the world around us. Tara Well's approach is smartly
based on science, yet her true gift is making these lessons accessible, personal, and even fun. This book is for anyone who wants to experience the
power of seeing themselves clearly and compassionately."

—**Tasha Eurich, PhD**, organizational psychologist,
and *New York Times* bestselling author of *Insight*
and *Bankable Leadership*

"*Mirror Meditation* is a game changer! If you ever struggle to believe in
yourself, *Mirror Meditation* will help you reconnect to your worth and
move forward to create a richer and more rewarding life."

—**Margie Warrell, PhD**, speaker, and author of *You've Got This*

"What happens in your mind when you look at yourself in the mirror? Drawing on psychological research and a deep understanding of human selfhood, Tara Well provides new insights into the nature of self-reflection. Her book is full of powerful stories, sage psychological advice, fascinating scientific findings, and provocative insights for living a full and authentic life."

—**Dan P. McAdams, PhD**, Henry Wade Rogers professor
of psychology at Northwestern University, and author of
The Stories We Live By

"What a gem of a book this is! Tara Well's *Mirror Mediation* is creative, fresh, and has the potential to bring great relief to many. The book is beautifully written, yet brings together research from social psychology to neuroscience. With clear exercises and tips for readers, it is a unique addition to the field of mindfulness, meditation, and psychology at large."

—**Robert T. Muller, PhD**, professor of clinical psychology,
and author of *Trauma and the Struggle to Open Up*

"*Mirror Meditation* is a very valuable resource, providing tools that are practical, easy to implement, and based on current research findings in brain science, health, and personality psychology. Its focus on increasing self-awareness, reducing self-objectification, and increasing mindfulness are timely and important in the era of Zoom meetings and seeing one's own face on screen all day. Tara Well is clearly an expert in her field, providing tools and research-based advice that is fresh, workable, and helps us relate to ourselves with greater self-compassion."

—**Melanie Greenberg, PhD**, clinical psychologist, and
author of *The Stress-Proof Brain*

mirror
meditation

The Power of Neuroscience *and* Self-Reflection *to* Overcome Self-Criticism, Gain Confidence, *and* See Yourself *with* Compassion

TARA WELL, PhD

New Harbinger Publications, Inc.

Publisher's Note

The content in this book is for informational purposes only and is not intended to be a substitute for professional advice, diagnosis, or treatment by a licensed mental health care provider. Seek the advice of a professional mental health provider with any questions you may have about your mental health.

This is a work of nonfiction. Nonetheless, some of the names and details of individuals and scenarios have been changed to disguise their identities. Therefore, any resulting resemblance to persons living or dead is entirely coincidental and unintentional.

NEW HARBINGER PUBLICATIONS is a registered trademark of New Harbinger Publications, Inc.

New Harbinger Publications is an employee-owned company.

Distributed in Canada by Raincoast Books

Copyright © 2022 by Tara Well
    New Harbinger Publications, Inc.
    5674 Shattuck Avenue
    Oakland, CA 94609
    www.newharbinger.com

Cover design by Sara Christian; Acquired by Jennye Garibaldi; Edited by Gretel Hakanson

Library of Congress Cataloging-in-Publication Data on file

Printed in the United States of America

24 23 22

10 9 8 7 6 5 4 3 2 1   First Printing

In memory of Richard

Contents

Introduction:
Explore Your Mirror Wisdom

Did you look in the mirror today?

Do you try to avoid looking at yourself?

Or maybe wish you could stop looking?

Mirrors can evoke some strong feelings in us. But they can also be incredibly useful in ways you might not have imagined. In this book, you'll find that the mirror is one of the most essential tools you have to deal with life's challenges. Because mirrors allow us to come face-to-face with ourselves. Being reflected is one of the most important and powerful experiences we can have as humans.

As adults, glancing in the mirror can become second nature. We use mirrors for personal grooming and to check how we look before we go out in public. But what if you took a different approach to how you see yourself in the mirror? Remember when you were a child? What was it like to see yourself in the mirror?

When I was a little girl, I used to look at my reflection in the side of the shiny chrome toaster on the table for as long as my parents would let me, clowning around, making faces, and imitating the adults around me. When I saw myself, I felt a sense of comfort and delight. But like most of us, as I grew older, society's expectations of me changed, and I started to use the mirror to scrutinize my appearance and compare it to the actors on TV and models in fashion magazines.

What I saw in the mirror never seemed to measure up.

Then one day, I caught a glimpse of my face in the mirror, and I was shocked by how sad and distressed I looked. I hadn't realized I felt that way. I'd been walking around thinking I felt "fine." In that moment of realization, I knew that, by trying to create a perfect image for others to see, I'd lost touch with how I felt inside. After that, I began to take time to look at my reflection in the mirror, not to focus on my appearance, but to simply acknowledge how I felt. Over time, it became a way to look beyond my appearance and see deeper into my own eyes with compassion. It became a meditation.

The mirror was so helpful to me, and as a research scientist, I wanted to understand why. So I began conducting mirror-gazing experiments in which research participants meditated on their own reflection. At first, they seemed awkward and self-conscious, their faces were often tense, and their eyes were harsh and critical. I guided them to see beyond their surface appearance and take a deeper look. In the process, something magical happened. Often by the end of the session, their faces had softened, and a glint of delight shone in their eyes. And, they reported some amazing insights. It was fascinating how a simple mirror could be the catalyst for so many different kinds of realizations. I worked with people and watched with wonder how meditating with a mirror changed them. They reported some amazing revelations. Three main changes stood out.

First, they became aware of just how much they criticized themselves. Whether it was their appearance or something else that they habitually found unacceptable, the mirror brought it to light. And the mirror revealed just how much their criticisms were affecting them because they could see it on their face! Then they had a choice, and a practice, to treat themselves with more acceptance and compassion.

Second, the mirror reflected their facial expressions with exquisite accuracy—so they were much more aware of how they were feeling moment to moment—which at first was a bit shocking for many. Some became more aware of emotions they typically avoided, like fear, anger, or disgust. Their capacity to accept and manage a broader range of emotions grew over time.

Lastly, a change I wasn't really expecting, but happy to find: many noticed a positive impact on their relationships. They became more aware of how they were seeing others and being seen. By practicing giving themselves their full attention, they were able to be more present with others, and their relationships deepened.

The mirror is one of the most valuable tools we have today. In a world of uncertainty, simply taking the time to look into your own eyes can calm you and awaken your kindness.

This book is a guide to seeing yourself and the world with clarity, honesty, and compassion.

The book is a progressive journey: you'll begin by learning how to find compassion for yourself in the mirror, discover calm in your reflection, and then apply this to connect with others. It is my hope that you'll take the many discoveries you make on your journey and live life reflectively. Now, let's begin the journey into deeper self-reflection with mirror meditation.

PART I

Facing Yourself—
Navigating Self-Awareness

1.   The Magical and Mundane Mirror

Mirrors are fascinating. This book is an invitation to transform your relationship with them. How you relate to mirrors may be more complex than you realize. So before we start the journey into mirror meditation, let's take a moment to consider some associations you may already have with mirrors. It's important that you understand how your past experiences and associations with the mirror might influence your self-discovery journey.

Over the past two hundred years, the mirror has evolved from a precious treasure that only the very rich could afford to an essential household item used daily worldwide. Almost everyone uses a mirror to do their grooming—shaving, hairstyling, applying makeup, and the like. The mirror allows us to see how we will look to others. Being able to take this perspective has great value. Our appearance is a cornerstone of our identity and the impressions others form of us.

Yet, the story of Narcissus warns against becoming too involved with our reflection. There are pitfalls of being too pleased with what we see. Throughout history, mirrors have been symbols of vanity, selfishness, and self-absorption. The wicked queen in *Snow White* asks the magic mirror, "Who is the fairest of them all?" A gauge of one's beauty is an aspect of the mirror that many of us know far too well.

In myths and stories throughout history, mirrors are potent objects of transformation and tools for trickery. Smoke and mirrors can obscure the truth. Like a magician's tool, the mirror creates illusions. Harry Potter sits before the magical mirror to see his deepest desires reflected and fulfilled. Why would he ever leave this comforting mirage? Unfortunately, mirrors can be powerful vehicles for self-delusion that hold us captive.

Mirrors are vital to your day-to-day functioning. In this section, you'll learn how reflections help you coordinate physically, emotionally, and socially. The mirror can also help us navigate self-awareness in some interesting ways. Mirrors simulate face-to-face contact with others, which is the foundation for how we relate to each other. After we discuss some of the fascinating ways to use the mirror, you can try a step-by-step guided mirror meditation that can become a daily practice. We'll also discuss tips for managing familiar sources of resistance to looking at yourself in the mirror.

- - - **try this** - - -

What associations do mirrors bring to mind for you? Use the following prompts to discover the associations that you already have with the mirror. You can write out your responses or say them aloud. For an advanced exploration, try saying them as you look in the mirror or video record yourself completing the sentence prompts. For each prompt, make an exhaustive list of responses. That is, keep going to pull for more and more associations. See if you can come up with at least twenty associations. Just write them down or say the first thing that comes to mind. There's no need to censor yourself or for your associations to make sense logically. The goal is to discover what kinds of associations and feelings you have related to the mirror.

For instance, for the prompt, "Mirrors are...."

One might respond:

Mirrors are mysterious.
Mirrors are exacting.
Mirrors are fascinating.
Mirrors are to be avoided.
Mirrors are tools for vanity.

And so on. You may be surprised at what comes through when you allow yourself to just freely associate without judgment.

Here are some other prompts to work with.

A mirror is:
A mirror reflects:
I like mirrors because:
I hate mirrors because:
In front of the mirror, I feel:

2. Going Mirrorless

The mirror is an essential tool for grooming, part of everyday life. Like many people, you may avoid looking at yourself for more than a glance to check for spinach or smooth a hair that's out of place. If you linger in front of the looking glass, you may reflexively start hunting for flaws. You might find that the mirror brings out your self-criticisms. So, why not simply avoid mirrors and the problem is solved?

Have you ever tried going mirrorless? Some have. Online blogs and articles document quasi-research studies and personal experiments of going cold turkey, giving up the looking glass.[1] These experiments have lasted for a few days to as long as six years. The accounts are strikingly similar. At first, people realize that the mirror triggers their self-criticism and appreciate having a break from it. Then, having to go to work or on a date during the experiment, they become insecure about how they look to others. They rely on a loved one for the spinach check and to tell them that they look just fine. As the experiment progresses, they tend to become less social: they start to feel awkward and avoid others. They also seem to miss themselves. The videos of mirror-deprived folks reuniting with their image reveal their delight. There they are! And they don't look so bad after all. The takeaway from these experiments is that it's not the mirror that's the culprit, but the thoughts and emotions it evokes. And, there's something essential about reflections in how we relate to ourselves and others.

You may not realize it, but mirrors and reflections play a fundamental role in your psychological and emotional functioning. The mixed feelings you may have about mirrors often reflect how you feel toward yourself. Instead of vilifying this harmless object, you can use the mirror to your benefit. Mirrors are incredibly powerful tools for self-awareness. You just need to know how to use them. Consider what the mirror can teach you. The mirror can demonstrate how little control you exercise over your attention and self-criticism. The mirror can be a tool to take back your focus and mindfully choose how you see yourself. You can learn to use these reflective surfaces more adroitly to increase your self-awareness with kindness. Please don't be afraid to look at yourself!

- - - try this - - -

1. How many times a day do you look in the mirror? Try counting. Find out how many times you actually look in the mirror within a twenty-four-hour period. Most smartphones have a counting function, so set it up and keep a tally of the number of times you glance in mirrors or reflective surfaces over the course of a day.

2. See if you can go a whole day without looking in the mirror. What feelings came up around the experience? When did you miss the mirror the most? When did you find not looking in the mirror to be a relief?

3. In the Beginning, There Was a Face

Have you ever been in a conversation and found yourself trying to catch someone's eye? You're talking away and suddenly realize that your companion isn't looking at you at all. It can be very disconcerting, in the least— and can even be downright painful to not be looked at or ignored. We seem to need their reflection as we express ourselves to them. Why is this so important?

Reflections are the foundation for forming a sense of self, learning to understand emotions, and relating to others. Our first reflections come from face-to-face contact. Faces are a unique focus for humans. We seem to have a natural draw toward them right from the beginning. Studies show that infants orient toward the face from birth.[2] For instance, newborns only nine minutes old were shown an image of a regular face or an image of a face with scrambled features. When the researchers moved the images along their line of sight, the newborns followed the regular faces longer than the faces with scrambled features. In their first few hours, newborns become adept at distinguishing between their mother's face and the faces of strangers. They look longer at images of their mothers than at images of other women. And within a few days, they learn to discriminate between different emotional facial expressions, like happy, sad, and surprised faces. During the first few months, faces become newborns' favorite stimuli as they acquire more and more expertise at identifying familiar faces. Newborns show a preference for direct eye contact too. Their response to faces continues to grow. So by five months old, they can match the image of emotional expression (for example a sad face) with its corresponding vocal expression (a sad voice). By five years, children's ability to recognize and label facial expressions is close to the competency of most adults.

Children develop self-awareness through early interactions. Caregivers imitate or mirror movements and emotional expressions and respond in ways that give them feedback that they are separate; children's behavior creates a reaction in others. It seems that we need a context outside ourselves to self-recognize. Other people reflect us as individuals, and mirrors do too.

Mirrors have proven to be essential tools to test for self-recognition and social awareness.[3] If you can tell that the image on the reflective surface is, in fact, you, then you have developed a sense of self. Children learn to recognize themselves in the mirror at around twenty months. Before that, they regard their reflection as either another baby to play with or something strange and suspicious. This kind of self-awareness is assessed scientifically by secretly putting a small mark or a lipstick kiss on a child's forehead, while the child is sleeping. The child can't feel the mark, so their sense of touch doesn't alert them to its presence, but they can see it if they look in a mirror. If the child has developed a sense of self, they'll reach up to touch the mark when shown a mirror, indicating that they know the mirror image with their own body.

As adults, we recognize our faces easily. Our face has a special meaning because of its importance for our identity and our sense of self. Research shows that our own face (called the "self-face") is recognized more quickly and accurately than the faces of other people we know.[4] This self-face-prioritization effect also occurs compared with familiar faces (such as family and friends). So, researchers have concluded that this effect does not happen just because your face is highly familiar but because it is personally unique information to you.

For instance, in one study, researchers showed participants their self-face so rapidly that it was only perceived below their conscious awareness.[5] They wanted to understand just how deep this special relationship goes. The self-face advantage was demonstrated at both the conscious level and the subconscious level. We are better at recognizing our own faces compared to the faces of others, even when the information is delivered subliminally—that is below the threshold of conscious awareness. They further found that seeing one's own face (more than seeing other faces) releases dopamine, which a neurotransmitter associated with feeling good.

So, looking at your own face can be rewarding—even if you're not consciously aware of it. Perhaps this is why many who practice mirror meditation find it so calming once they get over their initial conscious self-criticisms.

- - - try this - - -

1. If you are talking to someone on phone without any visual input from them, try looking at yourself in the mirror as you engage in the conversation. How does it feel to reflect yourself as you talk with another?

2. Think of the people in your life now and those you have known over the course of your life. Which of these people do you feel really saw you? Which of them did not? Describe in detail what it was like to be seen by them and not seen by them.

4. Reflections Are the Key to Coordination

Have you ever danced in front of the mirror? Or practiced greeting someone in front of a mirror before an interview or a date? We seem to know intuitively that reflective feedback can help us coordinate with others and our surroundings. The mirror provides a unique way to use our vision to orient ourselves in space. We need this reflective feedback to adapt and align ourselves with the ever-changing social environment.

Mirrors play a role in how you experience your physical body in space. A great example is exercising in front of a mirror. What actually happens when you exercise in front of a mirror? It depends on how you look at it. Mirrors produce different effects depending on your focus. Let's break down the most common ways you may be using mirrors in a fitness space and elsewhere, maybe without even knowing it.

First, the mirror is an excellent tool to check out your form. Of course, this is, at least in theory, the main reason mirrors are in gyms. In weight training and endurance sports, it's crucial to have the proper alignment to avoid injuries. And even outside the gym, we often use the mirror to check our posture and alignment. Maybe you've had the experience of catching your reflection as you're passing some reflective glass and noticed to your shock that you were slouching and holding yourself in a lopsided manner. You hadn't even realized it. Our bodies can get used to being out of alignment so much that we are unaware of it until we see our reflection. These distorted positions and patterns of movement can end up being the sources of injuries and chronic pain—unless we see them in the mirror and change them.

The mirror also allows you to see where you are in physical space and in relation to others. So this perspective is beneficial to dancers and actors who share the stage and need to move in coordination. With a mirror, you gain a broader perspective on your position relative to the group. But focusing on form and position can interfere with developing proprioception, which is the ability to sense relative positions of body parts without looking or thinking about them.

Proprioception is the internal focus on how your body senses as it's moving rather than how it looks. In general, research shows that *external focus* (focusing on how your movements affect the environment around you) leads to better performance than *internal focus* (focusing on how specific body parts or muscle groups are moving) during physical tasks. For example, free-throw shooting in basketball is better if you focus on the rim rather than on the movement of your wrist. In archery, you want to focus on the target, not the feeling in your biceps as you pull back the bow. External focus allows well-practiced movements to take place automatically without much conscious attention, which is more efficient than trying to control complex actions through mental effort directly.

So is looking in the mirror an internal or external focus? You could argue it either way. Imagine dancing with a partner who moves with you in perfect synchrony. You can use the mirror to practice your coordination by moving between an internal (proprioceptive) focus and an external focus on how and where your body is moving through space. With a mirror, you create a unique external focus. You're watching yourself from the outside.

Alternatively, mirrors can help you develop your internal focus by reflecting on the quality of your breathing and muscle tension. Use the mirror to check out the way you are holding your body: Are there areas of unnecessary tension? For instance, can you drop your shoulders or relax your jaw? Try observing your breathing pattern in the mirror: Are you breathing mainly in your upper chest or holding your breath as you move? Use the mirror to practice taking some deeper belly breaths. Research shows that slow deep diaphragmatic breathing increases concentration and present-moment awareness.[6] Deep breathing is also one of the quickest ways to reduce anxiety and calm yourself. So, when you see your reflection in the mirror in your favorite workout space, resist that urge to compare yourself with a superstar athlete. Instead, focus on your alignment, coordination, and breathing and use your reflection to focus and center yourself.

The research on phantom limbs is another excellent example of how mirrors help us connect to our bodies. A phantom limb is the sensation that an amputated or missing limb is still attached. About 60 to 80 percent of individuals with an amputation experience painful phantom sensations in their amputated limb. Mirror therapy can help people who've had limb amputations and nerve damage feel connected to their bodies again. How does it work? In addition to vision, we experience our physical body through proprioception, which is the perception of movement and spatial orientation arising from stimuli within the body itself. Experiments that use mirrors to create visual anomalies show that our brains crave consistency between vision and proprioception. For instance, arranging mirrors to make it look as if your left hand is actually your right will generally create a feeling of confusion and disorientation.

A mirror box with two mirrors in the center (one facing each way), invented by V. S. Ramachandran as an experiment, can help alleviate phantom limb pain. The patient sits with a mirror facing the remaining leg, moves the remaining leg, and watches the reflection in the mirror so that it appears that both the intact and the amputated legs are moving. In some studies, the technique has been found to decrease painful sensations in the phantom limb.[7] It seems the mirror creates a reflective illusion of the affected limb and tricks the brain into thinking movement occurred without pain. This fascinating research shows just how much we rely on reflections to gauge our experience. A glance in the mirror may be doing more for you than you realize.

- - - try this - - -

Sit in front of a mirror and slowly move a part of your body. Tilt your head slightly. Shift your focus from *looking* at your head tilt to *feeling* your head move. Raise your arm slowly. Watch it in the mirror. Then shift your focus to how your arm feels as it moves. Feel the air brush against your hand or the texture of your sleeve against you skin as your arm moves. Experiment with shifting your attention from watching your body move to feeling your body move. Notice the thoughts and feelings that come up as you shift back and forth from these two different states of self-awareness.

5. Two Sides of Self-Awareness

Mirrors offer insights into how we see ourselves. Self-awareness seems like a good thing because it allows you to know yourself, understand your motivations, and ultimately make better decisions. But it can also lead you to second-guess yourself and spin out into an excruciating state of self-consciousness, micro-analyzing every nuance of your thoughts and actions. The mirror increases self-awareness. Looking at ourselves for an extended period tends to evoke a level of self-awareness that many find uncomfortable. Why is this? How can we learn to navigate self-awareness so it becomes a source of information and compassionate self-awareness instead of a relentless magnifier of our every flaw and defect? Let's take a closer look at the two sides of self-awareness and see how they work.

First, internal, or private, self-awareness is a metacognitive process in which we take an observer's perspective of our thoughts. Internal self-awareness occurs when we become aware of some aspects of ourselves, but only in a private way. For example, you may notice that you can't stop thinking a particular thought. You may feel your stomach drop when you realize you left your phone at a restaurant or feel your heart skip a beat when someone you're attracted to enters the room.

Second, external, or public, self-awareness emerges when we become aware of how we appear to others. We take the perspective of a public observer. That is, you're aware that others can see you—and you may start to speculate on what you think they are seeing. External self-awareness often comes online in situations where you are the center of attention, such as when you're giving a presentation or talking to a group of friends. This type of self-awareness can compel you to act according to social norms, instead of how you feel inside. When you are aware that you're being watched and possibly evaluated, you're more likely to try to behave in ways that are considered socially acceptable and desirable.

Both types of self-awareness are necessary to maintain your sense of self and to navigate complex social interactions. For instance, in a conversation at a cocktail party, you need to be aware of your thoughts and feelings so you can decide whether or not to share them. You also need to be mindful of how others are perceiving you and reacting to what you're saying. However, certain habits of self-awareness can make you self-conscious.

Do you tend to be more internally self-conscious and have a generally higher level of internal (or private) self-awareness? If you focus your awareness internally, you tend to be more aware of your feelings and beliefs. So you may be more likely to stick to your values because you are acutely aware of how your actions make you feel. However, you might also tend to focus on your negative internal states, like unpleasant thoughts and body sensations. These negative internal states may then become magnified through intense internal focus and can lead to increased stress and anxiety.

Do you tend to be more externally self-conscious and have a higher level of external (or public) self-awareness? If you focus your awareness externally, you tend to focus more on how other people view you and are often concerned that other people might be judging you based on your looks or your actions. As a result, you might tend to stick to group norms and try to avoid situations in which you might look bad or feel embarrassed. So you might not take risks or try new things for fear of looking stupid and wrong in public. External self-awareness can also lead to evaluation anxiety in which you can become distressed, anxious, or worried about how others perceive you. Habitual intense public self-consciousness can lead to chronic conditions, such as social anxiety disorder.

Most times, the uncomfortable feelings of self-consciousness are only temporary and arise in situations when we are "in the spotlight." Most everyone experiences self-consciousness from time to time. Have you ever felt like people are watching you, judging your actions, and waiting to see what you will do next? This heightened state of self-awareness can leave you feeling awkward and nervous in certain situations.

How do you get out of an uncomfortable state of self-awareness? First, realize you have a choice on where you put your attention. Then, deliberately shift your focus.

If you are in a state of external self-consciousness, shift your attention off yourself onto others. For instance, if you are giving a presentation, focus your attention on your audience and building a rapport with them. Don't focus on yourself and how nervous you are or how you are feeling moment to moment. Focus your attention outward instead. In a conversation in which you start to feel uncomfortably self-conscious, shift the focus to the other by asking them an interested question. When we feel anxious, we tend to focus on ourselves, and that tends to make us even more anxious. In conversation, remember to volley the attention back and forth—don't hold the ball of self-consciousness.

If you are in an uncomfortable state of private self-consciousness, such as a self-conscious thought loop, shift your focus outward. Look at your surroundings, find something beautiful, find something blue. Play a game with yourself to see the world anew. Engage your senses: feel the texture of a velvet pillow, smell the grass, listen for a bird, feel the pressure of your feet on the ground and the air brush against your cheek. Expand your focus outward, and it works to take your attention off yourself and take a break from self-scrutiny. When you are in an uncomfortable internal state, you can lose sight of the bigger picture.

- - - try this - - -

One reason people often dread looking in the mirror is that it activates self-awareness. They do not realize that they can control their focus. You can practice shifting your self-focus from internal to external and back again as you look in the mirror. For instance, too much external self-awareness can lead to a self-objectifying perspective. Shift to looking at your face and checking in with how you are feeling in the moment.

Too much internal self-awareness the mirror might magnify an uncomfortable emotional state. Shift to the observer perspective, as though you are watching a friend experience this unpleasant emotional state. This is likely to evoke feelings of self-compassion. Take the observer's perspective by shifting your attention outward.

Becoming aware of your focus and developing agility in changing it can be helpful in navigating complex emotions and social situations with ease. We'll come back to this in later chapters on emotion regulation and connecting with others.

6. Facing Yourself Mindfully

What happens when you sit in front of a mirror for an extended period with no goals, no instructions, no specific intention? In other words, just *staring* at yourself. It can be painful! Increased self-focus without the deliberate qualities of mindfulness can lead to rumination, self-obsessing, and anxiety. It can create an uncomfortable state of self-consciousness instead of compassion.

Alternatively, some methods encourage people to say positive affirmations to themselves in the mirror. The self-help guru Louise Hay popularized the technique in the 1970s. The fictional character Stuart Smalley said mirror affirmations in comedy skits on *Saturday Night Live*. Talking to yourself in the mirror has its merits, as we will see in part 3. But it can also be a way to manipulate the experience of being with yourself and make you less aware of how you are genuinely feeling. Have you ever looked forward to seeing a friend after a hard day, and you just wanted to hang out and enjoy their company, but they could not stop talking, telling you how wonderful you are, how it was so nice to be with you, and on and on? Or you were feeling sad, and your friend kept telling you all the reasons you shouldn't be sad? It becomes annoying when we experience constant pressure to feel a certain way—even with ourselves. Sometimes saying affirmations can be like gaslighting yourself! We'll discuss gaslighting in depth later.

The mirror meditation in this book is first introduced as a silent practice. It allows you to discover what's present in the moment and how you truly feel without pressure to change it or gloss it over with a smiley face. The mirror meditation practice was developed based on the three key intentions of mindfulness meditation: attention to the present moment, open awareness, and kind intention toward oneself.

Being in the present moment means intending to keep your attention in the here and now. If you find yourself drifting off into thinking about what has already happened or imaging the future, you gently return to yourself and your reflection in the here and now. Remember, it's a practice in mindful self-awareness. Our minds naturally drift from thing to thing.

What differentiates an experienced meditator from a novice isn't how often their mind drifts, but how quickly and easily they can come back to the present moment. So, you practice simply bringing your attention back to yourself in the present moment, letting go of any self-judgments, and knowing that however you're doing it is quite all right.

Open awareness means intending to keep your focus receptive to whatever may arise in the moment. As you look at yourself, you may expect to feel critical but feel some delight instead or vice versa. Or you may see something in yourself that you hadn't seen before. Be open to experiencing anything and everything possible as you do the meditation. Let go of preconceived ideas about what should happen or even what you'd like to have happen during the meditation. You may be surprised by what comes into your awareness by simply being open to receiving without judgment.

Kind intention means to approach looking at yourself with an attitude of caring and respect—compassionate awareness. This is the essential element. Sociopaths usually have their attention focused in the present moment with open awareness for anything that might happen, though they definitely lack kind intention! Practice seeing yourself through kind eyes. Judgments about your appearance may come into your awareness. Looking at your image may evoke stories from your past. Strong emotions may arise. Whatever you're experiencing, remember to hold yourself with care, as you would a dear friend. And yes, I know it takes practice! When we practice holding these intentions as we look at ourselves, the mirror becomes a tool to transform self-criticism and self-objectification into self-acceptance and self-compassion.

- - - **try this** - - -

Sit in front of the mirror and practice the three aspects of mindfulness meditation. Use your own image to bring your attention to the present moment, be open and curious to whatever arises during the experience, and do your best to have a kind intention toward yourself. Of these aspects which do you find the easiest and the hardest? Why?

7. Ready to Try Mirror Meditation?

Here are five basic steps to start your daily mirror meditation practice.

1. ***Set the space and intention.***

    Choose a well-lit distraction-free space where you can position a mirror so it's freestanding and you can see into your eyes without straining or leaning forward. Sit on a meditation cushion or a chair with both feet on the ground. Set a timer for ten minutes. Have no goals other than to sit with yourself for the allotted time.

2. ***Tune in to your breathing.***

    Begin with your eyes closed. Tune in to your breath. Are you holding your breath or breathing rapidly? Take a few slow, deep belly breaths. Then breathe regularly and naturally, just observing your breath move your belly, ribcage, and collarbones as you inhale and then gently contracting your collarbones, ribcage, and belly as you exhale. Notice any areas of tension in your body, especially your face and shoulders, then imagine sending your breath to relax those areas and letting tension melt away.

3. ***Begin to gaze into your eyes.***

    Notice if your breathing changes when your first look at yourself. Come back to full steady breathing. Notice the quality of your gaze: Is it harsh or soft? Try to soften your gaze as much as you can. If you notice yourself hardening by focusing on a detail or a flaw in your appearance, breathe until you feel yourself softening again.

4. ***Observe your critic.***

    If your initial reaction to looking at yourself is critical, notice your eyes as you look at yourself in this exacting, maybe even harsh or cold way. Now see if you can flip your attention from the person in the mirror that you are scrutinizing to see the person underneath receiving that scrutiny. That's who you truly are. How does that part of you feel be receiving those critiques?

5. *Notice where your attention goes and the associated feelings.*

Gaze at your reflection, staying open to whatever arises. Notice any sensations or emotions that come up and allow them to be there without judgment or interpretation. Let your feelings and thoughts pass by as you breathe, relax your body, and gaze at yourself with no goal other than to be present with yourself. Notice if your attention becomes very narrow and exacting, and if so, see if you can expand it back to see your whole body, your whole self, and notice any emotions on your face. Observe this expansion and contraction of your attention and the thoughts and images that come to mind. Just see where your attention goes and the feelings that are associated with it without judgment. Hold a kind intention toward yourself as you do the practice. You may be surprised how much your view of yourself can change in ten minutes. Above all, be kind to yourself.

Many people find it challenging to look at themselves for ten minutes. You might find it hard to bear the amount of self-criticism that the mirror reflects in you. But remember: It's not the mirror being critical, it's you. The mirror is merely focusing and magnifying the quality of your attention on yourself. It may be illuminating your running commentary, stories, judgments, and so forth. All the ways your mind wanders in traditional eyes-closed meditation also happen in mirror meditation. And as in regular meditation, it may increase your awareness and intensify the habitual ways that your mind wanders. Meditating in front of a mirror is unique because you can see how these thoughts affect you by the emotions that show on your face.

If you find it too challenging to sit for ten minutes, start with a three-minute mirror meditation and work up to ten minutes—or look at yourself for as long as you can and then deliberately take a break and look away or close your eyes. You can come back to look after that.

8. Befriending Your Resistance

So, you're uncomfortable looking at yourself? Distraction is a common way to avoid discomfort. We all get distracted. I've noticed that people seem to have unique patterns that take them away from being present and having more of what they want at the moment. Seeing your pattern with compassion for yourself is the first step in changing it. Here are some common ways you may be resisting staying present with yourself during mirror meditation and some ways to counter them.

If you find yourself feeling spacey, try wiggling your toes and letting your feet sink into the ground. Some people even start to hallucinate when they do mirror meditation. There are, in fact, several esoteric practices that use mirrors to enter other states of consciousness. Psychologists who study perception have an interpretation of this phenomenon. They consider it a naturally occurring optical illusion called the Troxler effect. In any case, I'd encourage you not to trip out—intend to stay with it and to stay with yourself.

If you find yourself having the urge to flirt with or entertain yourself in the mirror, be compassionately aware of your social habit. Maybe you're used to feeling like you have to do something to feel good (or make others feel good). This habit may come from childhood conditioning or social expectations. In any case, see if you can let go of this impulse and stay open to what might happen if you do nothing. By letting go of your plan to feel or look a certain way, you may go deeper into your feelings. See what it's like to be with yourself and do nothing. Surrender the urge to manipulate the experience or change your mood.

If you're looking for something (or someone) to compare yourself to, you may be used to looking for affirmation that you're doing it right or *better* than others. Consider the possibility that there's no right or wrong way to do mirror meditation. And, if you're looking to compare yourself with some standard of excellence to feel worthy, maybe even superior to others, sorry, there's no better or worse way to do it. There's no need to compare yourself to others because there aren't any performance standards in this. So it's an excellent opportunity to let go of the comparison habit, take a break from competing, and just be you.

If you're feeling as if something's missing, you may have the urge to find out what it is. Consider the possibility that it could be you who's missing. You may be used to taking the third-person perspective—that is, imagining how you look to others—and when you stop doing that, it can feel like there's nothing there. I can assure you, there's a lot for you to discover inside. Try to let go of the urge to fill this empty feeling with something. Just stay present with yourself as best as you can. Nothing to do, just being with yourself. Treat yourself with kindness, be patient, and stay with it.

Each time you do mirror meditation, your experience is likely to be a bit different. I encourage you to stay with it—that is, to stay with yourself. Be patient and allow new ways of seeing yourself emerge in the moment, as you would when spending time with a beloved friend.

PART II

Your Beautiful Distraction

9. The Trifecta of Self-Cruelty

"I'd rather not look!"

"Can't stand these crow's feet."

"I looked so different when I was young."

"This gap in my teeth! So embarrassing!"

"I just keep noticing this enormous bulge."

"My one eye's bigger than the other."

"I didn't realize my ears were so huge."

When people find out I teach mirror meditation, they often say, "I hate to look at myself in the mirror!" Followed by one of three main critiques about their appearance. I've come to call this the trifecta of self-cruelty: "I'm too fat, I'm too old, I'm too ugly." This trifecta has infinite combinations and variations on the three themes, but they all have one thing in common: they're incredibly cruel ways to regard oneself! Studies find that 80 percent or more of people are not content with their appearance.[8] Looking in the mirror can serve to remind us of our imperfections.

In this section, we'll discuss why we often approach the mirror with a self-critical attitude. And why we tend to see ourselves as objects when we first look in the mirror. Then you'll learn some ways to use mirror meditation to deal with appearance issues. You'll learn to release self-criticism, shift out of an appearance focus, relax, and see yourself more deeply.

We have a built-in negativity bias, which is the tendency to see more negative aspects than positive ones. Negative features also tend to be more salient and emotionally impactful than positive elements. We have a more differentiated and elaborate vocabulary for negative stuff too. For example, you are more likely to say, "There's this small red bump on my nose," but when shifting attention to your positive features, you might say something general like, "My hair looks good."

Negativity is an attention magnet. For example, in experiments on impression formation in which the amount of positive and negative information is balanced and controlled, people will spend more time looking at the negative information.[9] When looking at negative information, research participants blink more. The blinking rate indicates more cognitive activity. They also show more significant increases in pupil diameter, heart rate, and peripheral arterial tone, all physical signs of more attention and alertness to negative than positive information.

Aside from studies of eye blinks, there is plenty of real-world evidence for this attentional bias. Bad news sells more papers, as in "if it bleeds, it leads," and the bulk of successful, engrossing novels and movies are full of adverse events and turmoil. In both the laboratory and the real world, there is convincing evidence that negative information generally has a stronger pull on our attention than does positive information. Why?

The reason our perception and cognition seem to work this way is that we need to be able to devote more attention and cognitive resources to potential problems. Our minds are naturally predisposed to look for problems as they can indicate threats and possible danger. When we look at something, anything really, without a clear intention to see the good or even remain neutral, we will automatically start scanning for problems, defects, and things that need fixing. Looking at ourselves is no different.

Due to a combination of evolution and socialization, our criticisms of the image we see in the mirror usually pertain to the three main topics: old, fat, ugly. We value youth, leanness, and beauty. Evolutionary psychologists tell us these qualities are a sign of reproductive fitness, and that drives our preferences and standards for perfection. By focusing on the supposed flaws of our physical appearance instead of how our harsh criticisms affect us, we perpetuate our suffering. Yet, it can be challenging to resist the urge to compare ourselves to the young, thin, beautiful human images we regularly see in the media.

10. Self as Object

When asked what they see when they look at themselves in the mirror, many people will recite a list of body parts, "My hair, my nose, my eyebrows," and so on. The mirror is the primary vehicle for admiring, scrutinizing, and critiquing these various aspects of our physical appearance. The mirror allows us to see how we will look to others. And, there are poignant messages and often great incentives to look as well-groomed and appealing as humanly possible. Being attractive is associated with a host of perks: earning more money, attracting desirable partners, and being seen as likable and intelligent. We associate beauty with success and all things good. Beautiful human images are everywhere to remind us of the value society places on our outward appearance.

Yet, there are real dangers in identifying too closely with our surface appearance. For one thing, it can lead us to monitor ourselves obsessively. We take a bird's-eye view and survey our bodies as we believe outside observers do. By placing such attention on dissecting how we look, we can easily forget about how we feel in the moment and as we move through life.

Have you ever noticed that when looking in the mirror for grooming, you may feel distant or disconnected from yourself, like seeing yourself without *really* seeing yourself? Viewing ourselves as we imagine we appear to others is known as self-objectification. We regard ourselves as a physical image—an object, instead of as an emotionally complex human. Self-objectification is encouraged and intensified by digitally perfected images in the media. We learn from a constant stream of images what society considers beautiful—and what it does not. Continuous exposure to these idealized images teaches us to objectify our physical characteristics and then compare them to these unrealistic standards.

Women are more prone to self-objectification than men because there are more social cues and social standards that communicate to women that they are being watched and evaluated based on their appearance. Surveys find that eight in ten women are dissatisfied with their reflection in the mirror.[10] It's not surprising. Media images of women retouched to perfection create standards of beauty that are nearly impossible to attain. The pressure to be thin, young, and sexy—but not too hot—seems to come from all angles. So when we look in the mirror, we see an image that needs fixing, rather than a real person suffering from self-criticism. When we use the mirror to check how we look, we can fail to notice how we feel.

Self-objectification is highest among teenage girls and decreases with age,[11] much like the social pressure on appearance women experience throughout the life cycle. Exposure to idealized media images increases self-objectification, along with anxiety, negative mood, and body dissatisfaction. Self-objectification is associated with lower self-esteem and depressed mood in early adolescent girls.

In one experiment, psychologists used a smartphone app to ping participants at random times during the day to report on their experiences.[12] They found that most women experienced events that triggered self-objectification daily and across a variety of contexts. These experiences negatively affected women's well-being, as indicated by their diminished feelings of vitality, positive affect, and engagement in the present moment.

In taking another's perspective, we, by definition, can't be in the present moment. Self-objectification reduces the frequency of flow states and diminishes cognitive performance. So if you want to reduce a girl's math score, have her do problems in a bathing suit with a bunch of fashion magazines lying around. Self-objectification also increases body shame, neuroticism, negative emotions, depressive symptoms, and creates a lessened awareness of bodily sensations and emotions.[13]

Researchers have used mirrors as an effective way to increase self-objectification.[14] In the classic swimsuit/sweater paradigm, research participants are randomly assigned to either try on a bathing suit or a sweater in front of a full-length mirror. As you might guess, those in the bathing suit group experienced more self-objectification than those wearing sweaters. It's true for women—and also for men asked to put on a Speedo.

Self-objectification reduces our awareness of bodily sensations and emotions too. We begin to see ourselves as "things" when we look in the mirror, instead of as real people. Many women habitually compare themselves in the mirror with idealized images in the media; this can intensify feelings of shame and anxiety. By putting so much critical attention on themselves, they may create their own suffering.

Self-objectification requires considerable emotional and cognitive resources. When we devote our time and attention to how we look, we end up having less attention for other concerns. Self-objectification has some interesting political implications too. For instance, a research project, called "Objects Don't Object," found that self-objectification impeded civic action.[15] Women who said they valued their appearance over their competence on a questionnaire were less likely to do things to promote women's rights and were likely to be content with the status quo. In another study, self-objectification was activated by asking female participants to recall a time when they experienced the "male gaze" in which they felt sexually objectified. Under these conditions of induced objectification, they were less likely to support women's rights issues and were more likely to think that the way things are now is how they should be. Together, these studies suggest, interestingly, that the cultural emphasis placed on women's appearance and the frequent sexual gazes they experience from men make it *less* likely for women to support their own equal rights.

11. The Neuroscience of Intense Self-Objectification

The use of mirrors for daily grooming often activates self-objectification as a default. It steals our attention away from being fully present, numbs our emotions, and distorts our self-perception. To examine just how impactful this is on even the most fundamental level, let's consider the case of pathological self-objectification known as body dysmorphic disorder (BDD). Most everyone self-objectifies to some degree, and most people have at least some aspect of their appearance that they'd like to change. But 2 percent of the population, men and women alike, has body dysmorphic disorder (BDD),[16] a mental health disorder characterized by a continued obsession with one or more parts of their body, causing severe distress that interferes with their daily functioning.

For those suffering from BDD, their physical flaws (real or imagined) come to rule their lives. This particular aspect of their body may be only barely visible to others or even nonexistent. BDD sufferers deal with symptoms that extend beyond unease when they look in a mirror. Some key features differentiate BDD from an average range of discomfort with one's physical appearance. First, BDD sufferers have a persistent preoccupation with a particular part of the body; common areas include hair, skin, nose, chest, or stomach. They can often dwell on a specific section of the body for hours and days on end. The believed defect might only be a slight imperfection or completely invisible and generally goes unnoticed by others. The preoccupation with the body part interferes with their daily life because they can't focus on anything but their perceived imperfection. Second, BDD sufferers experience social anxiety and tend to avoid social situations for fear that others may see their flaws and then ridicule and reject them. Finally, BDD sufferers perform compulsive or repetitive behaviors, such as excessive grooming, attempting to camouflage the fault with cosmetics, and seeking surgery and other physical alterations. These behaviors provide only temporary relief at best.

It turns out that BDD sufferers have some visual processing difficulties. So, it's not just that they *think* they have this flaw, but they *see* it in a distorted way when they look in the mirror. Brain-imaging studies have found disrupted face-processing patterns in BDD sufferers, including abnormalities in facial recognition and emotion processing.[17] That is, they appear to have an imbalance between what're called global processing and local processing. We have two components of perception that assist in identifying and recognizing stimuli. Local processing involves recognizing a stimulus by the individual features or elements, whereas global processing involves the overall form and relationships between features. Brain-imaging studies show evidence for one of the most common characteristics of BDD: the tendency to focus on specific details (local) of their appearance compared to their overall (global) image. BDD participants typically have abnormal patterns of brain activation when looking at faces. They focus on the tiny details of the face and can't really see the face as a whole.

This extreme attention to detail makes it difficult for people with BDD to recognize facial emotions. They have slower reaction times and reduced accuracy rates when asked to categorize faces by their emotional expressions. Specifically, they have a recognition bias in which they have greater difficulty identifying negative facial emotions, such as anger, fear, or sadness. And, they often interpret neutral faces as displaying contempt or disgust, which may relate to their fear of being criticized and rejected by others. Many BDD sufferers worry that they'll be criticized for their perceived physical flaws, which is escalated if, like many people with BDD, they also have social anxiety. So their fear of rejection seems to actually distort their perception of other people's facial expressions and impairs their ability to read emotional cues in social interactions.

An eye-tracking study looked at the visual-scan paths of BDD individuals as they categorized facial expressions by emotion.[18] They blinked more, paid less attention to the salient facial emotion features (for example eyes, nose, mouth), and had fewer long fixations and higher mean saccade amplitudes (indicating their eyes jerked around more). The patients with BDD used two general eye-scan-path patterns: "checkers," who would spend extended periods looking at particular facial features of concern to them, and "avoiders," who would look at nonsalient features of the face, such as the hair or chin.

When BDD sufferers look in the mirror, they have difficulty recognizing their own emotions. They may avoid being overwhelmed by anxiety and negative emotions by fixating on their perceived flaw. Their distorted perception may serve as a defense that guards them from feeling their most vulnerable and anxiety-provoking emotions.

Psychologists have attempted to alter how individuals with BDD sufferers perceive themselves using mirror-exposure and visual-training techniques. In these studies, the amount of mirror exposure is controlled, and participants are guided to shift their focus.[19] These interventions can be effective. BDD sufferers experience a reduction in their symptoms after mirror-exposure therapy. They were no longer fixated on their perceived flaw nor had such a negative reaction to their image.

Psychologists have suggested that BDD develops through the habit of prolonged mirror gazing. People use the mirror to practice looking at their perceived appearance flaw so intensely that over time, their perception becomes permanently distorted. So it's a bit of a chicken-and-egg conundrum: Is the mirror a creator or merely a reflector? Does the mirror create the body dissatisfaction and distortion, or does it merely reflect (and maybe intensify) the body-image issues already present?

Mirrors increase self-focus, and self-focus often activates our negativity bias, leading us to scrutinize ourselves and look for flaws as our general perceptual default. We have evolved to scan for problems and threats rather than to congratulate ourselves on everything that's going right. So, mirror gazing without a specified goal often leads to increases in appearance dissatisfaction even in those without body-image disorders.

12. Transforming Self-Scrutiny

We often feel alone in our self-criticism. A root cause of social anxiety is the fear of criticism. Yet, we are often our own worst enemies. A journalist once asked me, "What's the best remedy for body shame?" I said, "Don't shame yourself for shaming yourself!" Self-criticism is normal—everyone does it, and in moderation, it can be very informative in helping us improve. But it's essential to keep it in perspective.

I did a TEDx talk, which was a fantastic opportunity to share my work on mirror meditation, as I genuinely believe it's an idea worth spreading. But when I saw myself on the video, I recoiled: I looked, well, old, fat, and ugly! I felt the urge to hide, to crawl under a rock. It was pretty intense. Then I felt doubly ashamed. I'm "the mirror lady" who preaches self-compassion and self-acceptance, yet there I was having my own cringe-fest! I was supposed to be setting an example, after all! Ultimately, I realized it would be more self-absorbed and selfish to try and hide the talk because I didn't look perfect than to share my message and not worry so much about my appearance. It might sound simple, but that realization was tremendously healing for me.

Holding these self-critiques with kindness and clarity is the key to moving forward in life and reaching your goals—albeit however imperfectly. In the end, it is not how perfect you look but the quality of your contribution. Everyone I have ever worked with, be it a young, glowing supermodel or an average-looking middle-aged person, sees flaws in their appearance. We all have aspects of ourselves that we would like to change. Many people have poignant life stories of how their appearance for better or worse changed their fate. There may be some variability in the nature of these critiques. Still, the mirror always seems to reveal just how much their self-criticism is affecting them.

The mirror reflects the extent of our minds' unruliness and that our default is to look for problems. Mirrors may even magnify this process, but they can also be used to raise our awareness and slow the process down so we can see it more clearly.

At first, the mirror will shine a spotlight on your self-criticisms. If you intend to increase your awareness, you'll discover that you can free yourself from this criticism. You do this not by avoiding looking at it or pretending it's not there, but by intending to see clearly and change your perspective. You become more aware of how an outside stimulus like a mirror (or photo of a supermodel) can evoke your self-criticisms. Then you begin to have more control over where you'll let your mind roam and the emotions that come from your self-critical thoughts.

The mirror presents a golden opportunity to control your focus. You might be astonished to realize how much of your time and attention goes into focusing on how you look. Using the mirror with a clear intention is the key to seeing beyond your surface appearance and shining light on your inner critic(s). Looking at yourself in the mirror as a meditation will help you become more aware of how you disregard yourself through self-criticism and self-objectification. As you look at yourself for an extended period, you create a container, an exploratory space to become more aware of how you see (and don't see) yourself. It allows you to slow the self-objectification process down and identify the triggers of your self-criticism. You'll gain insights into how you see yourself and how it affects you. It's an opportunity to focus your attention on your image with open awareness and kind intention, let go of the scrutiny, and see yourself as you really are.

13. A Model Faces Herself

No matter how good our appearance looks to others, many of us still don't feel like we measure up. For instance, as a successful model, Clare took great pride in her appearance. She spent a fortune on all the latest cosmetics and hair products to make herself look and feel beautiful. Yet whenever Clare passed a mirror, some flaw always seemed to catch her eye. She became transfixed, her glossy lip curled in disgust, and she began scrutinizing face and body from every possible angle. It was painful to witness. To everyone else, she looked like a bright and beautiful woman. Her friends called her "Supermodel." Yet, despite the praise and attention she received from others and the amount of time and energy she devoted to her appearance, she was never satisfied with the way she looked.

When we started to work together, I suggested that she take a different approach to seeing herself in the mirror. I told her about the mindfulness principle of open awareness. The idea is that there may be other ways of seeing ourselves and things about ourselves that we have not discovered yet. As she looked at herself in the mirror, I suggested that she be open to the possibility of seeing herself in a new way. She practiced just being aware of her thoughts as she looked at herself without trying to fix anything.

It wasn't easy for her to do. Within a few seconds, she had a whole list of things she saw that were wrong with her appearance. She had a small pimple on her nose, her hair wasn't lying right, and on and on. I suggested that she take an observer's perspective and *simply watch herself criticizing herself* in the mirror. What was it like to see someone be disparaged like this?

This change in perspective led to a moment of realization. The shift in focus allowed Clare to become more aware of how much her critical thoughts were affecting her. She was able to shift her focus from seeing her supposed imperfections to seeing herself as the recipient of her own harsh judgments. She suddenly realized how unkind she was to herself.

It took practice for her to break the ingrained habit of looking through critical eyes. Eventually, she came to understand that she was creating her suffering because she could see it on her face. She then knew that she had the power to shift her perspective anytime—and the mirror could help her do it.

The mirror provides a way to externalize what's happening in our minds, so we have a different perspective and see how our thoughts are affecting us. For Clare, the mirror meditation wasn't about saying affirmations that she was beautiful to override her habitual criticisms. Instead, it was a practice that helped her realize how downright cruel she was to herself! She felt sad when she first realized the full impact that her criticisms were having on her well-being, and that motivated her to choose to treat herself more kindly. Her new attitude toward herself led her to treat others with more kindness too. And she discovered that she had more time to pursue her passions and things that mattered most in her life now that she spent less time and energy focused on her appearance.

As you look in the mirror, can you see yourself as the recipient of your criticisms instead of the object of them?

14. Looking at Aging and Invisibility

As a therapist in her fifties, Ann felt comfortable in the role of nurturer and support person. She was quite modest and even self-effacing at times. Taking selfies and looking in the mirror weren't her thing. Yet, she was intrigued by the idea of mirror meditation and thought it might be helpful to her clients. I agreed to show her the technique. After she canceled a couple of appointments, I met her for coffee to find out what was going on. She confessed, "I'm afraid to look at myself." As she grew older, Ann avoided the mirror as much as possible. She didn't want to see how her appearance had changed from the days of her youth. Ann didn't want to see her wrinkles, gray hair, and extra flesh. A cursory glance in the bathroom mirror was all she could manage. And even that filled her with a sense of hopelessness.

So the idea of *meditating* in front of a mirror was very much outside her comfort zone. She was content and believed it just wasn't for her. But something wasn't quite right about her objections. I noticed that Ann was a master at deflecting compliments. She did everything possible to avoid being seen. When I asked her about it, Ann confessed that as she grew older, she began to feel invisible. When she was younger, heads turned when she walked into a room. Now her presence often went unnoticed in professional and social settings. She felt a mixture of sadness and relief about it and just came to accept it.

She felt resigned that this was the time in her life to stay in the background and support others. I suggested she look at herself in the mirror with appreciation. She might want to see herself and acknowledge all she had been through in her life. I reasoned with Ann that we all have a basic need to admire others. And if the only people who let themselves be admired are those that meet an idealized standard of physical beauty or have self-interested agendas, it creates an imbalance. So Ann was actually helping her clients by being available to receive their attention, love, and admiration.

She came to see her self-effacing attitude as getting in the way of her good work. The mirror meditation helped her practice being more comfortable being seen and admired by others. Through her years of experience doing face-to-face psychotherapy, she modeled being an attentive listener, and now she no longer shied away from letting herself be seen and admired for her skill. Ann came to appreciate the power in the give-and-take of seeing others and being seen, and it elevated her therapy practice to a new level. She had a lot of wisdom to share with others, and her presence had great value for those who'd give her their attention. And she no longer shied away from making contact with new people. Ann began to realize how much her wise presence contributed to the lives of so many others.

After the age of forty-five, most women start to look in the mirror less,[20] and many experience becoming increasingly invisible by society. It may seem counterintuitive, but the mirror can be a valuable tool to navigate our complex reactions to the physical changes of aging. We can gain valuable insights into how we see ourselves and how others see us as we age.

15. Mirror Meditation to Accept Your Appearance

Instead of looking in the mirror and critiquing the image you see, practice awareness of your physical body as you look at yourself. Try this three-step mirror meditation with guided prompts to feel more centered in your body, comfortable in your own skin, and accepting of your appearance.

1. *Tune in to body sensations.*

   Set up your comfortable meditation space, sitting in a chair in front of the mirror. Take a few deep breaths and center into yourself. Gently close your eyes and focus your attention on your body, particularly the surface of your skin. Notice the places where your body is supported on a surface (like your thighs against the chair and your feet on the floor). Notice differences in the pressure of the parts of your body that are being supported against a surface and those parts that aren't in direct contact with another surface. Notice how the texture of your clothing feels against your skin. Notice the different sensations on your skin that is in contact with another surface or your clothing and on the parts of your skin that are exposed to the air. Feel the air brushing against your skin. Notice the temperature of your skin: Is your skin cooler or warmer than the air? Are different parts of your skin surface warmer or cooler? Once you feel you've tuned in to the sensations of the surface of your skin, move on to the next step.

2. *Practice progressive relaxation with body awareness.*

   Turning your attention to your breath, center into yourself. Then begin to relax each part of your body beginning with the soles of your feet, toes, and heels. Now relax your ankles, knees, and thighs, letting any tension drain out the soles of your feet. Notice your breath as you're relaxing your body and use your breath to create more space and ease, instead of holding your breath to try to get your body to do something.

Relax your hips, lower back, and belly, feeling your belly gently expand as you breathe in and gently contract as you breathe out. Your pelvis will naturally tilt back a bit as you breathe in and tilt a little forward as you breathe out. Imagine you're allowing your breath to breathe you. If you start feeling a little spacey, wiggle your toes and feel your feet on the ground.

Relax your rib cage and midback; notice how that area of your body gently expands and contracts with your breath. Relax the front of your chest and your upper back. Then relax your shoulders and upper arms. Notice if your arms or hands are holding or gripping. Are you holding something in your hands? Whatever it is (real or imagined), see if you can release it by relaxing your lower arms, wrists, hands, and fingers. Allow your arms to be fully supported on your lap and let any tension drip off your fingertips.

Bring your attention to the back of your neck and relax the muscles underneath your skull. Relax the front of your throat and relax your jaw by gently parting (or unclenching) your teeth. Notice how any tension in your jaw may be linked to your shoulders, arms, or hands.

Let all the muscles in your face relax, allowing your face to go completely slack and expressionless. Relax your chin, your lips, and your tongue. Relax your cheeks and the muscles behind your eyes. Relax the muscles between your eyebrows, your forehead, and your scalp.

Now coming back to your breathing, as you breathe in, notice any remaining tension and let it go as you breathe out.

3. *Practice an accepting gaze.*

As you breathe naturally, gently open your eyes and look at your reflection maintaining a soft gaze. Notice any changes in your breathing and muscle tension that occur in response to seeing yourself. Be compassionately aware of these reactions. And without self-judgment, simply relax and breathe, remembering that there's nothing to do but to look and see yourself and stay present with yourself.

Notice the quality of your gaze. Is it harsh or soft? Are you using your eyes to scrutinize and examine your appearance? Try to open your gaze to receive yourself. Let the image of yourself sink into your eyes softly. Notice your breathing; soften that too. Stay with yourself in this soft gaze for as long as possible. If you notice yourself hardening—focusing on a detail or flaw in your appearance—breathe until you feel yourself softening again. Receiving yourself as you truly are involves looking with kind eyes. Make a commitment to stay with yourself and practice simply observing and then letting go of self-critical thoughts about your appearance.

- - - going deeper - - -

Exercise 1. What labels do you use to describe what you're seeing in the mirror? Physical appearance? Personality adjectives? Say these words aloud to yourself as you gaze at your image. How does it feel? Do you notice any shifts in your awareness?

Exercise 2. Identify which media images trigger your self-criticism and self-objectification. Then take steps to limit your exposure to these images for a while and see what happens.

Exercise 3. Make a list of the ways in which you avoid being seen by others and put them in order from the least uncomfortable to the most uncomfortable. Do you dread being seen by others as fat, old, or ugly? Would you be horrified to be seen without makeup, unshaved, or hair askew? Which is worse? Are you willing to see yourself in those ways?

Exercise 4. A common question: What about saying positive affirmations, like "I'm beautiful" as you do mirror meditation? If you're feeling old, fat, or ugly and you smile at your reflection and say, "I'm young, thin, and beautiful!" over and over again, it'll definitely fill up the ten-minute meditation, and it may be helpful to avoid the discomfort of self-criticism. But, I encourage you to stay what's true for you in the moment. Don't gaslight yourself into thinking that you have to feel positive and look perfect whenever you look in the mirror. Ignoring how you're truly feeling can create resistance. Instead of escaping your discomfort with a positive affirmation, practice just staying with yourself, just observing, not trying to change or make anything happen. You may be surprised what you discover.

PART III

Witness and Choose Your Self-Talk

16. Why Is Self-Talk So Powerful?

Imagine you are walking down the street and see someone walking alone talking to themselves. You'd probably try to avoid them. Sometimes talking to oneself is thought to be the habit of eccentrics or a signal of mental instability. Yet, the truth is we all talk to ourselves. Have you ever been caught talking to yourself by a friend or family member? It can be embarrassing! Consider that you have an inner dialogue that's constantly running. Occasionally, you may accidentally blurt something out, but for the most part, this inner conversation happens in your head.

Our self-talk has a tremendous impact on our physical, emotional, and mental well-being. Yet, you may disregard it or at least underestimate its impact. You can use the mirror to explore your self-talk, saying your self-talk aloud as a regular part of the mirror meditation practice. In this section, we'll look at various forms of self-talk and experiment with some self-reflection exercises using the mirror and video. You'll get to know your patterns of self-talk, tame your critical voices, and cultivate encouraging self-talk for its maximum benefits.

Observing yourself in the mirror or on video creates a way to externalize your inner dialogue to see it from a different perspective. Yes, I realize this may seem a bit strange to see yourself talking to yourself. Maybe it brings up some apprehension as well. This is probably because for most of us self-talk sounds like self-criticism, self-judgments, and berating ourselves for mistakes or imperfections. With the mirror, you can face your inner critic, or critics, as many of us have more than one critical voice.

You are also going to begin making videos of yourself talking to yourself, for your eyes only! Why video? It's a powerful form of expression. Compare it to writing down your thoughts and feelings in a journal. Expressive writing, or journaling, illuminates our inner world of thoughts, feelings, and emotions. Research shows that it has been found to have many health benefits. We will explore how you can similarly use video journaling, with the added benefit of seeing yourself as you talk about things. On video, there is an immediacy and a spontaneity that is often lost when we have to stop and write things down. Using self-reflection, you'll gain an appreciation for the richness of your inner discourse, and from a broader, wiser perspective, you'll be better able to manage the committee in your head.

17. The Benefits of Self-Talk

The benefits of self-talk are numerous. In this section, you'll learn how to use it to your maximum benefit. For now, let's look at some research about what happens when your inner voices support you rather than hold you back.

Self-talk can enhance your cognitive performance. Self-talk may help your brain perform better. In experiments that measure cognitive performance, participants read instructions and then do the task.[21] Some participants read their instructions silently, others out loud. Results generally show that *reading aloud* helps us sustain concentration and improves our performance. In another study, participants completed a search task that involved visual scanning to find items.[22] Participants generally found the items faster when they *talked themselves through it,* which showed that self-talk can even improve visual processing. So if you're having difficulty with instructions to assemble a piece of furniture for instance, try reading the instructions aloud. If you can't find something, try talking yourself through it as you search for it.

Psychologists find that the beginning of self-talk in toddlerhood is associated with learning new motor skills, like reaching for objects and learning to walk, and later mastering more complex tasks, like tying shoelaces.[23] Some psychologists even believe that talking aloud when the mind is not wandering is a sign of superior cognitive functioning. So rather than making you crazy, self-talk can make you more intellectually competent. There may be some truth in the images of mad scientists talking to themselves, lost in their inner world of ideas. Maybe these geniuses are using self-talk to increase their brainpower.

Self-talk can boost your self-confidence. It's no secret that words of encouragement nurture self-confidence and self-esteem and increase one's chances for success. It works even when the encouragement comes from yourself! Researchers have found *encouraging self-talk* boosts performance across a range of athletics, from tennis to surfing and more.[24] In these studies, researchers divide the players into two groups. Both groups follow the same training program, but the experimental group practices self-talk. By the end of the training, the experimental group shows heightened self-confidence and reduced anxiety. And those who practice encouraging self-talk also improve their performance. We'll work with positive self-talk and the mirror later in this section.

Self-talk can help you manage negative emotions. You also can use self-talk to talk yourself down when you're in an upsetting situation. First, remove yourself from the dire predicament; then use self-talk to shift your perspective. Research shows that talking to yourself in the third person, as "she," "he," or "they" rather than "I," can be a particularly effective way to calm yourself down.[25] We'll explore talking to yourself from different perspectives later in this section.

In a research project to measure how changing perspectives might impact our emotions, researchers conducted two experiments.[26] In the first, participants were hooked up to an electroencephalograph (EEG), which measured brain activity, and were then shown images that varied from neutral to disturbing. One group responded to the images in the first person (for example, "I am finding this disturbing"). The other group used in the third person ("Tara is finding this disturbing"). The third-person group decreased their emotional brain activity much faster. In a second experiment, participants reflected on painful experiences while connected to a functional MRI machine that measured brain activity. Participants who reflected in the third person showed less brain activity in regions associated with painful experiences. These findings suggest that speaking to yourself in a way that gives you a bit of distance helps you calm down and not reexperience the event's pain when you retell it.

Self-talk is most beneficial when it serves a purpose or is goal-focused—and when it's done compassionately. Self-punishing ramblings are far less helpful and can decrease mental focus and exacerbate mental anguish. There are definitely times when instructional self-talk is not beneficial, like telling yourself to stop worrying and go back to sleep. Repeating the command to yourself like a mantra, "Stop worrying! Go to sleep! Stop worrying! Go to sleep!" is probably the worst thing you can do! Like any skill, to receive all the perks, you'll need to master the art of conversation with yourself. We'll be using our trusty mirror to do just that!

18. Exploring the Voices in Your Head: Uncovering the Inner Nurturer

You may discover that you have different voices inside yourself: some are kind and nurturing, while others are quite critical and harsh. The nurturers lift you up, and the critics drag you down. All these voices have a purpose. Your inner nurturer brings self-compassion[27] and encouragement, while your inner critic helps you recognize what you got wrong and what you need to do differently. But for most of us, the inner critic goes way overboard, exaggerating our faults, replaying them, and generating feelings of shame and self-reproach. Our inner critic seems so big and powerful, while our inner nurturer is often a tiny voice that's easily dismissed.

Uncovering the Inner Nurturer

How can we be realistic about ourselves and set the balance right? There are some tried-and-true techniques to strengthen the inner nurturer and tame the inner critic. Soon we'll use the mirror and video to get the voices out of your head where you can see them and work with them from a new perspective.

First let's explore your inner voices that are positive, good, and nurturing. In Buddhism and other religions, there is a concept of basic goodness. It's the assumption that everyone is basically good at their essential core being-ness. In other words, you were born that way: good. But through years of conditioning that focused on our flaws and the constant need for self-improvement, we can lose touch with our essential nature of goodness and derive our worth from our accomplishments and striving for betterment.

Bring to mind someone you feel is a basically good person. Not necessarily a saint. Just someone who has a basic sense of decency and caring. Then, start to make a list of people you consider to be basically good. Notice how you often almost automatically see the good qualities in others, even in people you might not know very well. Can you turn that around and remember that you are a good person too? Notice when others routinely acknowledge that *you* are a good person. Look for that in conversations: people who are happy to see you, trust you, ask your opinion, want to spend time with you, and so on.

You can choose to see yourself the way others see you, as essentially good and worthy. This might be hard to do. You may feel that it is taboo or too self-indulgent, maybe even narcissistic. But why not let yourself feel your goodness? If it's all right to see basic goodness in others and it's all right for them to remember it in you, why is it not all right to acknowledge it inside yourself? Can you be aware of the integrity and lovingness deep inside you? It might not always be apparent or expressed. Can you let a sense of confidence in your inherent value grow, fill your mind, and sink in? No matter what happens, you can always find comfort and strength in remembering that you're basically a good person.

- - - try this - - -

Think of the positive voices in your head. Consider that the voice (or voices) might not be yours but belong to those you have known who have reflected your basic goodness. Can you recall someone in your past who was nurturing and encouraging? A parent, a teacher, a therapist, friends, even a past love. What did they say that stuck with you?

You can strengthen the nurturing voice and sense of basic goodness by asking yourself, "What would my favorite teacher say to me now?" Take on the persona of someone in your life who was nurturing and encouraging and actually imagine what they would say. You may notice how much easier it is to do this with critical people and past experiences than for the kind nurturing voice. This is all the more reason to strengthen the nurturing voice and balance it out with mirror meditation.

19. Compassion at the Mirror

Now that you've located and started to become familiar with your basic goodness and the inner nurturing voices, we can begin working with the mirror to amplify them and discover more. This journey starts by becoming aware of the content and emotional tone of your internal dialogue when you face setbacks. Then you can intentionally make your self-talk more compassionate, encouraging, and nonjudgmentally accepting.

Having compassion for our own distress has been found to strengthen our ability to refocus and to soothe ourselves when we're feeling distress. You can intentionally activate self-regulation systems within you that create feelings of safety as opposed to feelings of threat and distress. These activities are self-soothing and stimulate positive emotions like contentment, safeness, and lovability—feelings that support caring and attachment. Yes, you can care for yourself and feel securely attached to you as your own caregiver!

Having compassion for our own distress has been found to strengthen our ability to refocus and consciously activate self-regulation systems that create feelings of safety as opposed to feelings of threat and distress. These self-soothing activities operate through the stimulation of particular types of positive emotions, like contentment, safeness, and lovability, that are associated with our innate motivations for caring and attachment.

In research, feeling safe is measured by increased heart rate variability (HRV).[28] This rate reflects how your sympathetic and parasympathetic nervous systems are balancing, which links with how you respond to stress.

If you have higher HRV, you have a greater ability to self-soothe when stressed and therefore have the capacity to act compassionately. Higher HRV actually inhibits distress-related reactions of fighting with or withdrawing from suffering. So you can engage with the suffering in yourself and others.

Mirror meditations can amplify compassionate self-talk. Compassion involves our hardwired self-regulation system that enables us to approach suffering instead of fighting or fleeing—that is, we orient outside of ourselves to see suffering and are then moved to act to alleviate it.

Psychologist Nicola Petrocchi and colleagues conducted a study to find out if using the mirror enhances the effectiveness of compassionate self-talk.[29] The research participants were asked to generate four phrases they would use to soothe and encourage their best friend. Then they were asked to describe an episode in which they criticized themselves and were assigned to one of three conditions: (1) to repeat the four phrases to themselves while looking at the mirror, (2) repeat the four phrases to themselves without the mirror, or (3) look at themselves in the mirror without repeating the phrases. Here are some examples of compassion phrases:

- *The parts of yourself that you don't like are parts of you that need your attention and love.*

- *You've been strong in the past, and you will be able to find your strength now too.*

- *I'm here, and I will be here forever; I'll always try to help you in any way possible.*

- *Think about all the positive things that you did and will do.*

The results of the study showed that participants who said the phrases in the mirror reported higher levels of soothing positive emotions. They also had more HRV compared to participants in the other two conditions. So it appears the mirror does boost the soothing effects of compassionate self-talk.

In the same way, compassionate self-talk can be amplified by the use of a mirror because it externalizes the object of your compassion: yourself. Also, in the mirror you can eye gaze and relate with facial expressions, which evoke your empathic responses. You'll be working with your facial expressions in the upcoming sections.

- - - try this - - -

1. As you look at yourself in the mirror, simply notice the general emotional tone that your reflection evokes in you. And see if you can have compassion for your lack of compassion.

2. Make a list of positive, soothing, compassionate phrases or sentences that you would say to comfort a beloved friend or those phrases and sentences that you'd most like to hear when you're feeling upset or down. Then say them to yourself in the mirror during a mirror meditation. How does saying them to your face feel?

20. Exploring the Voices in Your Head: Taming Your Inner Critic

Now that you've located the inner nurturer and are equipped with practices to strengthen your compassionate voice, you can start to explore other less-friendly voices, namely the inner critic. If you tend to be overly critical of yourself, you're not alone. Most people experience self-doubt and harsh self-judgment if not constantly, at least from time to time. But, you don't have to be a victim of your own verbal abuse. Instead, you can take steps to proactively address your negative thoughts and develop a kinder and more helpful dialogue with yourself.

First, understand that all the voices in your head are there for a reason. The inner critic's purpose is to protect you. Discovering this can be liberating. So let's explore the protective quality of your inner critic.

As with the inner nurturer, you may find that the critical voices belong to someone else like a parent, teacher, boss, or a former lover. These voices may be with you, constantly offering their critical commentary. Or it could be a friend or stranger who made an offhand remark that cut so deeply it stayed with you for years. The critical voice might be more general.

Consider the quality of the voice:

- Does it have a gender?

- Is it older or younger than you?

- What are its motivations?

- Is it trying to protect you or warn you of some danger?

- Does it simply want to humiliate you and keep you in your place?

- Is it direct and sure that you are or have done something terrible?

- Is it indirectly introducing uncertainty and doubt about you and your plans?

For instance, you may have a voice that says something like, "Remember *never* do or say that again!" This message probably comes out of an experience in which you did or said something that caused you physical or emotional pain. Maybe you fell and hurt yourself at a moment when you were feeling very confident, so now your inner critic warns you that it's dangerous to be too sure of yourself. Perhaps you made a fun, lighthearted comment to someone who had a snarky comeback that cut you to the bone. Your inner critic registers it as *"Remember never say that to anyone again!"*

In these cases, we could say that your inner critic's purpose is to protect you from experiencing this pain and discomfort again. But instead of protecting you as your inner nurturer might, it ends up hurting you all over again through self-punishing messages. These abusive messages can also generalize so that doing or saying anything spontaneously might be considered highly dangerous and grounds for retribution and lead you to feel fear and anguish.

The critic often speaks in absolutes, with little room for nuance or gray areas. Its favorite words are "should," "always," and "never." "You've screwed up it, just like you always do." "You should just quit; you're never going to win at this." "You're so different from other people; no one will ever want to be with you." "You've got so many issues to sort out; you'll never be able to fix yourself, let alone help anybody else." Sound familiar? Instead of creating hope and new possibilities in your life, the inner critic causes you to question your worth and makes your actions seem doubtful and ineffective.

Mindful self-awareness can help you see that the inner critic is actually preventing you from being in the present moment. It's either in the past, warning you to never do that again, or it's in the future, telling you that you are too flawed and not ready to move forward until you are perfect. There is often a repetitiveness to these messages. If you try to resist these self-critical voices, it may seem to make them even stronger. Instead of treating your inner critic as an enemy, try to consider it an ally. But one that needs to be checked and balanced. See the inner critic as attempting to help or protect you—but in a covert, distorted, or maladaptive way. This perspective makes it possible to connect with the critic and transform it over time into a helpful ally.

- - - try this - - -

When that critical voice pops up, see if you can balance it out by activating your inner nurturer. I call this the "Slinky exercise," named after the ancient spring toy. Sit in front of the mirror, and do some basic relaxation steps as discussed earlier, such as deepening your breath and shifting awareness to body sensations. Then rest your hands on your lap, palms up. Call to mind any situation you are struggling to resolve that is lurking in the back of your mind. Then imagine your inner critic in one hand and your nurturer in the other. As you imagine that you are shifting the Slinky back and forth, shift your awareness from one hand to the other. Notice that the two thoughts are connected by the Slinky as you shift your focus and the weight of your thoughts from one hand to the other. Say your thoughts aloud as you gaze at yourself with your imaginary Slinky resting in your palms.

Here's an example dialogue you might have if you are struggling with saying something you might regret in a meeting.

Inner-critic hand: "You screwed up! Now they think you're crazy!"

Inner-nurturer hand: "You're feeling regret about saying this—that means you care about yourself and others. That's so good. "

Inner-critic hand: "They're never going to forget that one!"

Inner-nurturer hand: "You'll have other conversations with them. There are many options: you could apologize or clarify what you really meant to say."

Inner-critic hand: "You've totally alienated everyone with the one incredibly stupid remark!"

Inner-nurturer hand: "They may be more forgiving than you think—even if they don't understand, I do."

And so on. Keep going so you express all the thoughts you have in both hands. Once you have the two distinct voices going, see if you can actually feel the weight of the thoughts of your critic and nurturer as you hold them in your hands.

Getting the voices out of your head, embodying them in your hands, and seeing yourself alternating between them in the mirror will create a shift. Oftentimes, your view will shift from watching a person who screwed up to watching a person who's suffering. It's easier to feel compassion for your suffering.

As you shift the weight of these different thoughts, remember that they are not separate, but linked as opposite ends of the Slinky. As you shift from one hand to the other, imagine you are weaving the two sides together, two-sides of a coin, or two ways of looking at the issue. Moving the Slinky in your hands will help you see the common theme. These hand movements can be very soothing too, especially if you've worked yourself up with a lot of self-critical dialogue.

In the example situation, the inner critic is trying to protect you from being ostracized or rejected by others: it wants safety and to trust responses when communicating with others. The inner nurturer wants the same thing, but it realizes that this can be had without always saying and doing things perfectly. So, both sides want the same: to feel safe and to trust yourself, to be liked by others, and to be included and appreciated by them.

So look for what your inner voices have in common. This will help to befriend the inner critic and not be so afraid of it. This exercise will help you balance your attention and remember your goodness. It's not about denying your mistakes, but if you keep going over them, analyzing them, and creating stories about them, you're just reinforcing the pain that they've already caused you. By recognizing and reflecting on the good aspects, you build a bridge to a place of kindness and caring. Sitting in that place increases your ability to look honestly and directly at whatever is challenging and gives you the confidence to move forward.

21. Ways to Express Your Inner Voices

Now that you've gained some awareness of different aspects of your self-talk, we are going a step further in the exploration. Self-reflective video journaling is a great way to take control of your self-talk and understand the patterns of your inner dialogue at a more profound level.

You may be familiar with making videos to post on social media and watching videos of your friends. But video journaling is different. It's like a video diary for your eyes only. When we make videos to show others, we tend to monitor what we say and do because others are watching. The whole point of making videos is often to show them to others and get a reaction. This kind of performance activates our sense of public self-consciousness discussed earlier. Video journaling is about revealing more of your true self—to yourself. Being open to exploring aspects of yourself you might not be familiar with is an asset here.

Let's compare video journaling to free-form expression writing. There is an exercise called "the Morning Pages," which was introduced by Julia Cameron in *The Artist's Way*. This exercise involves writing out longhand three pages of whatever thoughts come to mind first thing in the morning. I've found it tremendously helpful. For years, I sat at my table with a cup of coffee and wrote my three pages. Most of what I wrote was not terribly profound or exciting. And I certainly wouldn't have wanted anyone else to read it! Sometimes I wrote about things that were bothering me. Other times, I wrote about what I wanted to eat or buy at the store. I wrote about the death of a friend, food allergies, noisy neighbors, love interests, regrets, my budget. Whatever popped into my mind, I wrote it down. I noticed that it cleared my mind for the rest of the day. No matter what creative project I was working on, the ideas flowed much more smoothly after doing the Morning Pages. And, it definitely helped me to see my inner dialogue in a new light!

Our inner dialogue often feels like we can't really control it: thoughts simply pop into our head, and we can't seem to stop thinking them. These internal voices rob our attention and play havoc with our emotions.

Expressive writing can provide a framework to hold your inner dialogue. When you write down your self-talk, it's easier to see the patterns.

Research shows the healing benefits of expressive writing. Psychologist James Pennebaker conducted studies in which people recorded their "deepest thoughts and feelings" about a stressful or traumatic life event over the course of several days.[30] Encouraging people to write about their emotions had therapeutic benefits. It improved their ability to adapt cognitively and make meaning out of stressful life events. Researchers have found that expressive writing is linked to a wide array of psychological and physical health benefits. In fact, it's been discovered that the people who improved the most initially told very emotionally messy accounts of their stressful event—the more negative and disorganized it was, the better—then, as they wrote about the same event over a period of days, their narrative became more and more coherent. They seemed to develop more distance, perspective, and compassion for themselves. In contrast, those who told tighter, less emotional, more "together" accounts from the get-go didn't improve as much.

In a sense, expressive writing follows a course similar to psychotherapy. The therapist holds a space for you to get messy and vulnerable and articulate your true feelings about what's happened in your life. You might go over the same adverse life event many times. By listening and reflecting back to you, the therapist provides continuity and perspective, which, over time, allows you to integrate the experience into your memory so it's no longer sticking out like a traumatic sore thumb but simply another meaningful part of your unique life story.

Imagine you had a pop-up therapist on call 24/7, one who would immediately appear to listen to you with full attention, compassion, and clarity whenever needed to help you to manage your self-talk. Now imagine that person is YOU. You can use video journaling to tell your stories and then watch yourself telling them. It's not quite the same as expressive narrative writing—and it's clearly not the same as talking to a therapist—but this unique approach has some significant benefits. Giving voice directly to our inner dialogue may preserve its spontaneity while having the same psychological benefits as expressive writing. And, video journaling is available to you anytime.

Video journaling is a valuable tool for self-awareness and self-compassion. I know that watching yourself on video can often be nerve-racking and may activate your inner critic, but the rewards of seeing yourself from this unique perspective are enormous. I discovered this somewhat by accident during a particularly stressful time in my life when two of my close relationships ended, and I was too busy to do the Morning Pages. I began to make short videos of things I wanted to say to someone who understood me. Over time it became just as satisfying to tell them to myself—and sometimes better—because I didn't have to deal with others' reactions to some of the provocative things was saying! I used video journaling to recap my experiences of the day, to savor and amplify wonderful experiences. But I also talked about things that bothered me that I felt I couldn't share with others. I worked out my feelings by talking about them, and I saw how I was feeling by watching my recordings. I felt something significant had changed in me. I was no longer *practicing* self-compassion; it simply upwelled in me from seeing myself in these videos.

As I thought about it, it seemed that the videos provided a new way to see myself, to accept myself, and to stay with myself no matter how I was feeling or what I said. Having the recordings allowed me to look back on myself and my struggles with greater understanding and compassion. Everything and anything I wanted to say I said in my video journal. The process allowed me to practice being aware of and accepting all my moods and thoughts. Watching my videos helped me accept my imperfections and develop a stronger, more positive relationship with myself.

As I began teaching the practice to others, I discovered that many different people find video journaling to be a powerful tool for kinder self-awareness. Taking the time to express your emotions and then giving your full attention to watching yourself will help you integrate and process your feelings. This is great to do when no one's around to listen to you deeply or when what you have to say is confidential or might upset others. By making a private video journal, you create an intimate space for yourself to process your feelings, thoughts, and emotions without having to worry about others' reactions. You create a space to be honest with yourself and to see yourself being honest. From this practice, you can create a stronger and more positive relationship with yourself.

22. How to Do Self-Reflective Video Journaling

Now it's time to do it! You're going to use your smartphone, computer, or other video recording device to make spontaneous, unfiltered ten-minute recordings of yourself that will be seen only by you. Here are some tips for doing it.

- Make sure all notifications are turned off before you start.

- Make a plan not to share your recordings with others. You'll want to keep them private and secure. This will help you feel more comfortable because you won't need to worry about what others might think of what you're saying and feeling in your videos. You may find great freedom in not having to monitor yourself as you might typically do in conversation.

- You can talk about anything that is on your mind without concerns about the others' reactions. Try not to censor yourself. If you feel critical or self-conscious, then talk about that. Talk about anything that is on your mind or that you're experiencing in the moment.

- There's no way to do this wrong. Remember that the purpose is to practice seeing yourself, not to entertain others or to get them to see you or like you.

- Plan to make your video journal at a set time and place every day. Many people like to do their mirror meditation first thing in the morning and then do their video journal at night.

- If you don't have access to a completely private space, consider making the video journal while you're outdoors or in a semi-public area, though not ideal, it'll appear as though you're on a video call with someone when you're really making a video journal; people will be less likely to interrupt you.

- Even if you meet with inner resistance or outer logistical challenges, keep going. Your first few videos are likely to feel awkward and strange. This usually happens when we try something outside our comfort zone.

- Make your videos with no goal other than to be present with yourself. You don't have to look perfect, entertain yourself, or be working on improving yourself somehow. Just hang out with yourself and have a chat. Make a cup of tea, turn on your video, and catch up with yourself.

Once you've made a batch of videos, you might be curious to see what they like look. Since most of us have an aversion to seeing ourselves on video, it's essential that you watch your videos mindfully. Plan to watch your videos privately without any distractions: turn off all notifications and don't try to multitask. Do some of the deep breathing and body awareness exercises described earlier to center yourself and bring your attention to the present moment. Set your intention to be open to seeing yourself from this new perspective and activate your inner nurturer to support you in seeing yourself with compassion. Simply watch each video-journal recording at least once with your full attention and be aware of your emotions and bodily sensations as you are watching yourself. Don't make any plans for self-improvement!

By watching your video-journal recordings mindfully and in their entirety at least once, you'll become aware of various emotions and habits of speaking and recurrent thought patterns that you may not have previously been aware of. You may want to make a specific time every day to watch your videos. You will find that watching them immediately after you have made them is different from watching them several hours or days later. You can watch your videos a day, a week, a month, or a year or several years later. You'll be fascinated by how much you change and the insights you will gather about yourself!

Remember, this is simply a practice in seeing yourself with new awareness. There is no way you can do it wrong. Your self-reflection practice is perfect every time you do it. And remember to be kind to yourself!

Exercise 1. Begin and end your video journal with a clear intention. Some examples of clear intention at the beginning might be to be honest and to give the experience your full involvement for the ten minutes. You might end your video by articulating something you're grateful for. Or, imagine you're speaking to a dear friend. How would you begin and end the conversation?

Exercise 2. Try making videos in a different tense. Make some in the first person, "I feel great today"; the second person, "You're feeling great today"; and the third person, "Tara's feeling great today." How does it feel to use these different perspectives, and what is it like to watch yourself?

Exercise 3. Make time to review your videos. Prepare your space, breathe and ground, and watch your videos with a kind intention from this open, relaxed space. What insights come to mind? What do you see when you look at yourself? What is the primary emotion? In what ways do watching yourself on video change your view of yourself?

PART IV

Beyond Selfies and Looking for Likes

23. Sign of the Times

As we learned in part 3, video journaling is a great way to increase your self-awareness and understand yourself in ways you can't get to by introspection alone. Watching yourself tell an emotional life story or experience a feeling you hadn't known was inside you can be so powerful. It can help you grow and strengthen your compassionate relationship with yourself.

This section will discuss some of the common ways that our social world, particularly social media, can disrupt your progress to understand yourself compassionately. We touched upon messages around beauty and appearance in part 2. Here we focus on how social media influences your attention and how your social media habits can keep you from developing the capacity to listen to yourself and others deeply.

As our world is becoming more digitized, we're spending increasing amounts of time on our devices. Even before the pandemic, Americans spent an average of eleven hours per day looking at screens.[31] Yet, when we look at our screens, we are not looking at ourselves—or each other.

A notable exception is the Zoom experience, the explosion in video conferencing ignited by the worldwide pandemic. Many people felt "mirror anxiety" around seeing their face on the Zoom call—so much so that people developed an aversion to video calls. It became crystal clear that many people do not like looking at their own reflection. There are many reasons for this reaction. We discuss some here and then explore being seen and seeing others in depth in later chapters.

Let's compare the Zoom experience with taking selfies. Why would selfies be so popular but seeing yourself on video much less appealing? For one thing, you don't have as much control over your image on video as you do when you post a selfie. You can take a hundred selfies and select the one that's perfect or edit it until it is. On Zoom, you can't control your image or other people's reactions to it. Instead, you see their reactions to you in real time. You may have experienced "Zoom fatigue," that stupor-like feeling you get after a full day of Zoom calls. Zoom fatigue occurs when your brain has to work extra hard to process all the facial expressions that are up close and out of context on video calls. In contrast, you can post a selfie and count the likes, which is much easier than trying to decipher the complex nonverbal cues in real-time engagement.

In terms of emotional satisfaction, connecting with others on social media is just not the same as connecting in person. Posting a selfie and getting likes is not the same as showing up in person at a social gathering and getting smiles and warm hugs.

Taking more than three selfies a day is considered an actual disorder by the American Psychiatric Association. Although selfies might seem harmless, there is a strong relationship between selfie addiction and various mental health issues, like poor self-esteem, narcissism, loneliness, and depression, especially among young people.[32] It is one thing to warn us of dangers, but it may be better to know how to meet our needs for social connection and belonging in more satisfying ways.

Taking selfies and posting them is socially isolating in itself. Research also shows that people do not look favorably upon those who post a lot of selfies.[33] So despite getting likes, if you post a lot of selfies, you might actually be harming your social standing and relationships. Selfies may create the illusion of social connection and popularity. But think about it: a selfie is you being alone trying to get others to like you.

Selfies are often less about being seen for who you truly are. They are more about image control. They may be attempts to make connections with others, but they often miss the mark. Selfies can come from an urge to be noticed and liked by others. But research shows they can end up creating more anxiety and depression.[34] We can spend more time looking at our screens and looking for likes than in face-to-face contact with each other. As a result, we're missing out on the face-to-face reflection that is so important to our social and emotional functioning.

In this section, you'll learn why it's so easy to get hooked on taking selfies. Then we will discuss how mindfulness meditation can help with addictions. Next, we'll adapt this approach to mirror meditation. Two case studies will show that there are different needs behind taking selfies. Finally, you'll learn how to use mirror meditation to shift away from the urge to take a selfie and develop more compassionate self-awareness of your true needs.

24. Selfie Addiction

Sarah went on vacation to the tropical island of Aruba. She wanted to get away from the hustle and bustle of her life in New York. She saw a beautiful sunset and wanted to capture the moment. So, she took a photo of herself with the warm orange, pink, and blue sky behind her. It looked great. Then she got the urge to post it on Instagram. She thought of a cute caption and hashtag and felt even more excited. As she pressed the button, she felt a boost of pleasure. Then she headed off to meet her new vacation friends for dinner.

On the way, she felt compelled to stop and duck behind a palm tree and check her phone to see how many likes and comments she'd received so far. Once she finally arrived at dinner, though happy to see her friends, she could hardly focus on the conversation. Her mind was on her Insta post: Many likes? Who commented? What should she say back? She knew she had to comment back or otherwise, it'd be rude, and more comments help the algorithm so more friends and followers will see her photo. But if she replied too soon, she'd appear desperate, but if she didn't respond soon enough, her friends might forget about her post.

After dinner, her friends suggested a walk on the beach. But Sarah decided to go back to her beach hut and look at her Instagram feed instead. Maybe she should post another selfie from earlier in the day. But she realized that she needed to edit it to get the color just right, make herself look thinner, and accentuate her facial features. Again, she felt excited, thinking that the second photo would get even more likes and comments!

What makes us compelled to take selfies and post them instead of just enjoying being in the present moment?

In *The Craving Mind*, psychiatrist and mindfulness and addiction researcher Judson Brewer uses the basic principles of rewards and punishments to help us understand addictions. There are three steps to the process of becoming addicted to something:

1. We feel an urge to do something rewarding that makes us feel good, called the *trigger*. Triggers can vary from person to person.

2. We engage in the *behavior.*

3. We receive the *reward.*

So applying this to Sarah, her brain—just like your brain—takes in information through her five senses. For example, she sees a beautiful sunset. Based on similar experiences, her brain interprets this as pleasant or unpleasant. In this case, it says, "I like this sunset!"

If pleasant, her brain gets an itch or an urge: "I want some more of that!" If unpleasant, it says, "Get this stuff away from me!" So we are motivated to act in ways that make the good stick around and make the bad go away. For example, you post a picture on Instagram, and you get a bunch of "likes" and comments about it.

If your behavior was successful, your brain lays down a memory to remember to do it again in the future. "That was great. Don't forget to take more pictures and post them when you see a beautiful sunset on exotic trips!" So now, when you see something beautiful or cool, that becomes the trigger. This trigger-behavior-reward sequence goes on and on to sustain a wide array of addictions, including selfie addiction.

What's more, a neurochemical response—the dopamine hit—becomes part of the reward. It is what makes the reward rewarding! Dopamine is a chemical produced by our brains that plays a prominent role in motivating behavior. Dopamine gets released when we taste delicious food, when we have sex, after we exercise, and, importantly, when we have successful social interactions, including when we receive likes on social media. Dopamine makes us feel good, and it stimulates more reward-seeking behavior.

Let's start to unpack what makes us get hooked on selfies. This particular addiction relates intimately to mirrors, social reflections, and our self-image. We can understand the basics through the trigger-behavior-reward sequence. The triggers can be seeing something you like, the behavior is associating yourself with it, and the reward is getting likes and comments on social media.

For instance, you pass a lovely fountain on your way to the dentist. The fountain is the trigger motivating you to associate yourself with beauty or distract yourself from thinking about the dentist. The behavior is taking a toothless smiling selfie by the fountain and posting it. The reward is receiving likes and comments, further distracting you from your dental experience.

Or, you might feel envy at a friend's selfie in which she looks so thin (trigger) and decide to take a similar photo of yourself and to edit and shave off a few pounds (behavior) to get the rewards in the form of comments, "Wow, you look amazing!"

The trigger could be feeling bored or a vague sense of emptiness. The behavior is posting a fun, kooky selfie to see how your friends will react to it, which stimulates your curiosity and increases your dopamine, so you feel good; that's the reward.

- - - **try this** - - -

There is great variety in the number of trigger-behavior-reward patterns we can fall into over time. Take a moment to reflect on your patterns. Can you identify your triggers, behaviors, and rewards that are unique to you?

25. Ideal Images Versus Self-Reflection

As we saw in the case of Sarah, her compulsion to take selfies and post them robbed her of opportunities to enjoy the precious moments of her vacation. Her preoccupation with selfies created a stubborn obstacle to making new friends and enjoying their company in real time. We also learned how insidious the selfie habit could be because we can train ourselves to get dopamine hits from our selfies. How can we break the selfie habit and get our social needs met in deeper and more fulfilling ways?

Mindfulness techniques are very effective in helping us slow down the trigger-behavior-reward sequence so we can understand ourselves better and choose whether to act on our urges. As with most addictions, the behaviors that started out incredibly rewarding end up becoming routine, mindless habits. When we take a mindful approach, we can stay present with ourselves through the process, and the shift in perspective can be the foundation for change.

In the case of selfie addiction, psychiatrist Judson Brewer suggests four steps for increasing mindful self-awareness. The steps form the acronym RAIN taught widely by meditation teacher and psychologist Tara Brach and originally developed by senior meditation teacher Michele McDonald.

Recognize/relax into your urge to take a selfie or post one.

Accept/allow it to be there; don't resist it.

Investigate bodily sensations, emotions, and thoughts right now.

Note what is happening from moment to moment without attachment.

You can use RAIN in your mirror meditation. Imagine your urge as a wave that you can ride. You can learn to ride the waves of wanting by surfing them in the mirror. For example, if you feel a strong desire to post a selfie, the first step is to *recognize* it and *relax* into it. You have no control over it coming. So *allow and accept* this wave as it is. Please don't ignore it or distract yourself. Don't try to resist or do anything about it. Just look at yourself with a soft gaze as you are having this experience.

Find a way that works for you. Consider a word, phrase, or gesture that acknowledges that you agree to go with this wave. For example, try a simple nod at yourself in the mirror. Consider a soothing gesture, like stroking your hair or gliding your thumb across your fingertips, acknowledging that you consent to go with this wave of wanting with a kind intention toward yourself.

As in surfing, to catch the wave of wanting, you have to get to know it by *investigating* it as it builds. Engage your five senses. Be curious. As you gaze, ask yourself aloud, "What does my body feel like right now?" Don't go looking for things. Just see what arises most prominently. Let it come to you like a wave. Open your five senses to what you're experiencing moment to moment.

Finally, *note* the experience as you follow it. Please keep it simple by using short phrases or single words, for instance, "thinking," "restless stomach," "shoulder ache," "burning," "tightness," "heart racing," "itchiness," and so forth. Follow the wave until it completely subsides. If you get distracted, return to yourself by repeating the question, "What does my body feel like right now?" Be open to your experience changing moment to moment. There are no right or wrong ways to do this.

You can practice RAIN in front of the mirror and make a soothing gesture as you begin the wave. Ask yourself aloud, "What does my body feel like now? Where is this wanting in my body?" As you face yourself and your urge, you'll gain more control and self-compassion.

Then it may become easier to ride the wave of wanting to post a selfie, check your phone, or whatever when it's not convenient to plop down in front of a mirror and meditate. The soothing gesture will become associated in your mind and body with allowing and accepting your urges and sensations, but not with acting on them. You can then ride the wave of wanting anywhere and anytime. And, over time, the craving will subside in intensity.

You can use this technique with any type of urge you may have that you'd like to be better able to manage, such as phone checking, snacking, smoking, sexual behavior, and so on. The first step is to identify the urge or craving. Then you must be willing to face yourself with awareness and compassion.

26. Trying to Maintain Image Control

We live in an image-based culture. Many people feel pressure to create a personal brand. In fact, it's not uncommon to see ourselves as a product. We are the food in our social media feeds. Technology makes it easier and easier to share images of ourselves as soon as the urge arises. With built-in editing software and links to numerous sharing platforms, it's quick and easy to edit, crop, colorize, and share. With all the filters available, it's always possible to portray your ideal self or better! A flattering photo can make you feel good and increase the number of likes you get, making you feel even better. That creates a dopamine boost, and pretty soon, you're addicted to the cycle.

I met Ali through a mutual friend. She was a well-known influencer with an impressive Instagram following. She made a six-figure income endorsing products on her social media platforms. She created images that linked her beautiful, sexy, smiling face and products like cosmetics, health food, even kitchen gadgets.

She was getting burned-out and had tried traditional meditation practices but found herself too antsy and impatient to develop a regular practice to get the benefits. Ali was so oriented toward her image from honing her brand. So her friend thought mirror meditation might work for her.

When she arrived, I was a bit shocked at how different she appeared in person. She looked exhausted, older, and heavier than her photos. Her facial features were also strikingly different. She picked up on my surprise and said, "I know, I know, all my selfies are beautified!" She further explained that she was starting to turn down opportunities to participate in live events because of the discrepancy between what she actually looked like and her online image. On the one hand, she liked having her business entirely online, but on the other, it was also socially isolating. She was thinking of getting extensive cosmetic surgery to alter her face and body to look more like her "beautified" Instagram photos.

I asked her to describe her experience of taking selfies and posting them. She explained that she had been doing it for years. At first, she enjoyed posting and getting likes from her friends. Then her appetite grew, and she needed more and more likes to be satisfied. The likes and comments were rewarding in themselves, so was watching her number of followers increase steadily. Then brands started contacting her with endorsement and partnership offers. As her online presence and bank account grew, she devoted less and less time to living the healthy lifestyle she had been promoting when she started. So, Ali started to doctor her photos, at first, just to look a bit more well-rested and glowing. Then she started editing to look taller and thinner. Then she began editing to make her nose and waistline more petite. Then she felt she had to make her lips, eyes, and bust look larger, and on it went.

The more she altered her image to resemble a perfect beauty, the more likes, comments, and online opportunities came her way. She now had a whole team of people working for her whose job it was to beautify her online photos. Now, she was burned-out and wanted to take some time off and get back in touch with herself before deciding whether to have cosmetic surgery.

As she sat in front of the mirror, she automatically started smiling and posing. She wanted to take a couple of selfies, "Just a couple before we start," she pleaded, "we can fix them to look good." Seeing her own image immediately triggered her wanting to take a selfie.

So I suggested we dive right in and ride the RAIN wave. I encouraged Ali to allow herself to feel the urge and just observe it. "I feel so antsy, like I am going to explode if I don't post this!" We did some deep breathing and grounding practices to help her relax into the urge. I asked her where it was located in her body. "My heart is pounding. My hands are itching to pick up my phone. Now I am getting flushed—this is embarrassing," she said. I noted the excellent tracking of her physical sensations. I suggested she create a soothing hand gesture to do instead of reaching for her phone. She tried rubbing her thumb against her fingertips and breathing deeply. She said she felt foolish and embarrassed that she had this urge so strongly. I explained later that this was a learned pattern and she had been practicing and strengthening for many years, so she had to be patient with herself.

I worked with her to use the mirror to ride the RAIN wave of wanting to post a selfie. At first, it was challenging to identify the urge because it seemed constant and even accentuated by seeing herself in the mirror. It was as though she was living her life on Instagram. She believed that every image and angle was an opportunity to take a selfie. It took a few sessions for her to start to see herself in the mirror without looking through the lens of Instagram selfies. Finally, she began to let go of the idea that she had to be creating value for others at all times. I encouraged her to be open to looking at herself with curiosity and to just hang out with herself and practice doing nothing.

Eventually, Ali discovered some intense self-judgments about doing nothing and the belief that she somehow had to be contributing to everyone's experience at all times or else she wouldn't be liked or accepted or worthy of attention. She traced this back to her childhood when her parents told her to smile and act pretty or people wouldn't like her. Ali found that when she looked in the mirror, it intensified the power of those early messages. So I encouraged her to be compassionately aware of her self-judgments and see if she could let go of the impulse to create something to give to others and be open to what might happen if she stayed with herself and just did nothing.

By riding the wave of her urges to take selfies, post them, and check for likes, she was able to let go of seeing herself as a product to be liked. She learned to have compassion for herself. She was slowly able to let go of the desire to manipulate her image and others' reactions to it. Ali learned to be content to be herself however she was feeling in the moment. In this practice, she made a private space to explore her deepest emotions without producing for others. She created intimacy with herself. Spending time with herself just hanging out doing nothing became deeply nurturing for her. Over time, she started to relate to others in a more relaxed and genuine way. Her authenticity attracted new friends and deeper, more rewarding relationships, based more on internal qualities, like acceptance and kindness, and less on physical appearance.

27. Attempts at Emotion Management

Not everyone feels pressure to create beautiful selfies. Katrina didn't think she had any issues with her appearance. So she posted outrageous selfies all day long: with and without makeup, smiling, crying, grimacing, licking the camera lens, you name it.

She recognized that her selfie habit was starting to affect the quality of her work and her relationships. We first needed to identify her triggers. Sometimes she posted selfies when she was bored and just wanted to stir things up. She also felt the powerful urge to post a selfie when she had a strong emotional reaction to something. "I just don't know what to do with myself, so I post, and then I get all this love back immediately." She came to see me for mirror meditation instruction because, despite all the "immediate love" she was receiving in the form of likes and comments, she felt lonely, and her emotions were getting out of control.

I asked Katrina about her daily activities. She worked at a high-paying tech job where she felt invisible. She used a pseudonym on her social media accounts, so only a select few friends knew her true identity. She spent much more time interacting online with people she really didn't know than with friends and family face-to-face.

It was clear to me that Katrina was not getting enough face-to-face interaction with others. Lack of face time with others who cared and would listen was making it more difficult for her to manage her emotions. She was instead trying to use selfies to validate her feelings. But, unfortunately, this was not really working for her for several reasons.

First, she had created a persona that hid who she really was. So, on the one hand, she did not have to risk being rejected or judged for how she felt. But she also didn't have a way to get acceptance for who she really was and what she was feeling in the moment either. Her friends on social media didn't actually know her personally.

And none of it was taking place in real time. Katrina did not have the experience of seeing firsthand how her so-called friends were actually responding to her. She received likes and comments, "I know how you feel,"

"Sending so much love," and tons of heart emojis. But these were shallow substitutes for the actual face-to-face intimacy that Katrina craved.

She was so emotionally open and vulnerable on Instagram. Although she longed to be loved and accepted by true friends, the thought of sharing so openly with them was just too scary to consider. She did not want to be laughed at or judged as emotionally unstable.

So, I asked her to try an experiment: whenever she felt the urge to post a selfie, she should instead turn her camera on herself and just look for two or three minutes. Katrina had a tendency to exaggerate her facial expressions to show her emotions in her selfies. So, I suggested that she try to be still with a neutral expression on her face as she looked at herself. This exercise turned out to be quite challenging for her. By giving herself her own attention instead of trying to get attention from others, she uncovered a well of deeper emotions that she'd been trying to avoid by posting her outrageous exaggerated selfies.

She found a good therapist she trusted and worked out her feelings in private. She stopped taking selfies and did mirror meditation regularly instead. She used the mirror as a tool for support between therapy visits. It helped her focus on how she felt inside and treat herself with kindness and respect. She started to realize how much she had been negatively affected by her Instagram feed. Spending so much time online was making her socially isolated. So Katrina decided to cultivate more genuine relationships and meet regularly with her friends for face-to-face conversation. Mirror meditation helped her feel more comfortable being seen by her friends, and she saw them in a new way too—not as potential "like" givers, but as real people who cared. Over time, her relationships became deeper, more intimate, and mutually respectful and supportive, and less about posting provocative selfies.

PART V

Tame Your Anxiety
Through Reflection

28. Facing Anxiety

When I first learned to drive, I'd hit the brake every time I felt the slightest apprehension. I didn't realize I was doing it. Until one day, I took my Siamese cat to the vet. She was already pretty anxious. Every time I hit the brake, she let out a blood-curdling wail. Through my cat's reaction, I learned that I was much more anxious than I realized—and that my anxiety was affecting others around me.

Many times we don't realize how anxious we really are until someone points it out. In case you don't have a Siamese cat around to reflect your anxiety, I'll show you how to use the mirror for feedback on your own anxiety, without becoming more anxious in the process. Together, we'll explore what anxiety is, how anxiety grew out of our brain's basic survival mechanisms to become a self-perpetuating habit, and how you can see it differently and respond to stress more effectively.

The dictionary says that anxiety is a mental and physical state of negative expectation. It's a feeling of worry, nervousness, or unease, typically about an upcoming event or something with an uncertain outcome. That can describe almost anything! It seems like anxiety is pretty common. In fact, it is.

When you combine fear and uncertainty, you get anxiety. When you anticipate situations that could lead to bad or dangerous outcomes and you aren't sure what to do, you feel anxious. Like before a job interview or a first date, when you get invited to speak in public or have your taxes audited, or when you travel to a new place. When we get ready for major life changes, like going to college, getting married or divorced, or having a child, even positive changes, it can create anxiety. We are headed into the unknown. It can feel uncertain and scary.

Anxiety can show up in many forms. However, some typical symptoms of anxiety are edginess, restlessness, tiring easily, lack of focus, irritability, increased muscle aches, and difficulty sleeping. Symptoms vary so much from person to person. That's why anxiety can sometimes be so hard to recognize, especially in ourselves.

Fear is the basic emotion that underlies anxiety. Fear is the emotion that helps us survive. Fear warns us of danger and readies our body to fight, flee, or freeze in the face of threats. These responses prepare the body to deal with immediate threats to our survival, like the saber-toothed tiger in the old days. As life became more complex, our brains did too. We developed a prefrontal cortex to help us plan and think up creative solutions to problems. We are now very good at thinking about and planning for the future. For instance, we've become very skillful using our brainpower to imagine worst-case scenarios to prepare for possible threats in the future. Unfortunately, this type of brain activity can also generate a good deal of anxiety. Our imagination can be the prime creator of our anxiety. Some degree of planning for negative outcomes is necessary; however, much like the inner critic, the part of your brain that worries can go way overboard.

Anxiety is meant to capture your attention and motivate you to make the necessary changes to protect yourself and the things you care about. So occasional bouts of anxiety are natural and can even be productive. Anxiety is part of being human and having the ability to anticipate and imagine what is meant to happen. But persistent, pervasive, or out-of-proportion anxiety can disrupt your daily life, whether at school, work, or with friends. Nearly one-third of adults in the US will face out-of-control anxiety at some point in their life.[35]

Anxiety is usually a private affair that happens in your mind. Regularly experiencing anxiety can make it more difficult to recognize your emotions. If you're constantly in a state of anxiety, you might be experiencing too much fear and high arousal to notice other emotions. If you have anxiety, especially social anxiety, you may spend less time out socializing with others. You can miss out on the face-to-face feedback that would help you be more aware of your feelings and better able to manage them.

As children, we learn to understand our emotions and control our reactions through face-to-face contact with others. Other people's reactions to our emotions teach us a lot about how to understand our feelings. We continue to need this kind of reflection throughout our lives. Unfortunately, as we spend more time alone and on our devices, we miss this essential mirroring. Lack of mirroring is a factor in the growing number of people with general anxiety disorders and social anxiety disorders. These disorders manifest as persistent worrying about doing or saying the right thing, the inability to tolerate uncertainty, difficulty concentrating or relaxing one's thoughts, as well as difficulty recognizing one's own emotions.

In an intriguing set of studies, psychologist Piergiuseppe Vinai and colleagues used mirrors and video technology to help people with anxiety recognize their own emotions through "self-mirroring."[36] They learned to soothe themselves in the mirror when they felt anxious and others weren't around to offer reflection and support.

This section will elaborate on the concept of self-mirroring and show you how to use the mirror for self-soothing and to calm yourself down when you're feeling anxious. We will also discuss how anxiety influences how we see the social world generally. Then we'll explore the fight, flight, and freeze responses to threats. I'll show you some self-reflection techniques to get out of these uncomfortable states so you can cope with challenging situations more effectively.

29. What's Driving Your Attention?

As our world becomes more digitized, we're spending increasing amounts of time on our devices. Even before the pandemic, Americans spent an average of eleven hours per day looking at screens.[37] There is a positive relationship between screen time and anxiety.[38] We don't know whether increased screen time causes more anxiety or whether more anxious people are online for more extended periods. Probably it's a bit of both.

Many of us spend more time looking at our screens than in face-to-face contact with each other. As a result, we're missing out on the face-to-face reflection that is so important to our social and emotional functioning. Concurrently, loneliness and narcissism have increased, while examples of empathy and compassion often seem in short supply. The number of people reporting anxiety and depression has hit an all-time high.[39] Those struggling with anxiety and depression often have difficulties recognizing their own emotions and have significant deficits in cognitive regulatory abilities, such as focusing attention in the present moment.[40] As technology becomes more sophisticated in its ability to grab our attention and stir our sentiments, it is becoming more and more vital for us to maintain our autonomy and decide for ourselves where we wish to focus our time and attention.

We have a limited capacity for attention—that is, there are always many more things in the environment trying to grab the spotlight than we could give our attention to. So how do you choose what is worthy of your attention? And, how much free choice do you have over it? We have a natural tendency to focus on the things that threaten us—as in the negativity bias. Threats and dangers automatically pull our attention.

Attention is considered the primary commodity in the attention economy. To sell something, be it a product, an idea, or a service, we must first secure the potential buyer's attention. Pumping our newsfeeds and media outlets with negative news, exaggerating problems, and then selling solutions are time-honored marketing and persuasion techniques. "If it bleeds, it leads" is an old saying attributed to newspaper editors; it's how your brain works too. In a sea of information, your brain will pick out the scariest bits and focus on them. That, of course, creates anxiety.

When we feel anxious about something that is not an immediate threat to our survival, we often seek to gather information about it. Hence, the internet rabbit hole is born.

What are the most common topics that generate anxiety? Those related to our survival. According to the research,[41] the most common anxiety-provoking topics are concerns and uncertainty about money, health, conflict in relationships, and public events or performances.[42] This list reflects our survival concerns: we care about our resources, the physical and mental well-being of ourselves and loved ones, and our degree of social connectedness and acceptance from others.

Everyone is concerned with survival and aims to live a threat-free life. But, we each have our own unique triggers. What are yours? In a day or a week, take note of everything that makes you feel anxious. See if you can make a list of triggers. Be specific. Here some examples.

Getting an email about a credit card

Not getting a reply to an email or text

Getting stuck in traffic on your way to a work meeting

Being asked to give a presentation

Going on a first date

Confronting a neighbor about a noise issue

Saying no to a friend's request

Seeing your boss giving you a weird look

Having a suggestion rejected by your partner

You may notice that most of the items on your list are challenging but not life-threatening. Make a video journal about your anxiety triggers. Try talking about them in the first, second, and third person. How does the change in perspective shift your anxiety?

30. Anxiety Can Distort Your Vision

A question for you: Can you be curious and anxious at the same time?

Anxiety creates a heightened state of arousal. Your body gets geared up for some imagined threat or challenge. This reaction automatically shifts your perception to maximize your ability to deal with the threat. Thus, being in a state of anxiety regularly can change how you see yourself, the world, and the people in it.

Anxiety can change your visual perception in complex ways.[43] We've discussed the negativity bias earlier. Our visual attention is biased toward noticing possible threats in the interest of self-preservation. So, on the one hand, research shows that anxiety heightens our senses. Our hearing is keener, and we see farther distances when we're anxious. But on the other hand, anxiety also narrows our focus, giving us tunnel vision, which can make it more difficult to see situations accurately. You may have seen extreme cases in movies where the character becomes paranoid and thinks everyone is out to get them. The camera distorts the images to show how the character's mind is being twisted by paranoia and suspicion.

When you're in an anxious state, the mirror can play tricks on you. Because, in a sense, you can see double in the mirror, and that can double your anxiety. You want to avoid feeling as though you're looking into a fun-house mirror. So it's generally not a good idea to stare directly at yourself in the mirror for an extended time when you're in an anxious state.

Instead, ground into your body. Practice deep breathing, tap your fingers together, slap your thighs, wiggle your toes. Feel your physical self.

Do some compassionate self-talk. "I'm okay." "You can stop and take a moment to relax and breathe." "Tara can slow down and deal with this one step at a time."

Then pay attention to your eyes. Are they narrow or open? When we're afraid, we open our eyes wide to find the threat and signal potential danger to others. When we see the threat (real or imagined), we narrow our focus, zeroing on it so we can closely monitor and plan to attack it.

Psychiatrist and mindfulness researcher Judson Brewer created an exercise to help you shift out this narrowly focused state of anxious attention.[44] He reasoned that by understanding how your eyes connect to your emotions, you could learn to tap into curiosity to help you shift out of fear and anxiety. Brewer suggests opening your eyes really wide as a way to jump-start your curiosity. (I recommend first experimenting with this without looking directly in the mirror.) Next, keep your eyes open really wide for ten seconds, and notice what happens to your anxiety. Does it get stronger or weaker? Does it change in character or shift in some other way?

- - - try this - - -

Consider opening your eyes really wide for ten seconds after you've been scrolling, texting or typing, or watching images on your devices for a good while. It can create a feeling of refreshment for your eyes and mind, shift your perspective, and quickly get you out of any rabbit holes.

31. Self-Mirroring for Self-Soothing

When you're feeling anxiety, you can use the mirror to soothe yourself. Research shows that traditional meditation practices can work well to help reduce anxiety[45] Using the mirror may increase these benefits. There are three main components of meditation that you can use with the mirror to relax and soothe yourself: breath control, body awareness, and mental focus.

Breath Control

Reflexively, when you are feeling anxious, your breathing changes. You may start to breathe rapidly, or you may hold your breath. Think of preparing yourself to rip a Band-Aid off or being in a social situation where you had to stop yourself from laughing (or crying). Chances are you held your breath in an attempt to stop yourself from feeling. A sudden shock elicits a reflex of quickly sucking in the air and holding it. If we sense a threat in the environment, we instinctively hold our breath to stay still and not make a sound. You can get in the habit of holding your breath without realizing it when you're feeling anxious or worried. Anxiety can also cause you to breathe shallowly and rapidly. Either of these changes in your breathing can make you more anxious.

You can take control of your breath. Slow deep breathing is one of the quickest ways to calm yourself down. In the mirror, focus on your body. Watch your collarbones and rib cage rise and fall with your breath. If looking into your eyes makes you feel more anxious, then just focus on your body. If you are breathing fast, tap your fingers together slowly or tap your feet on the floor to help ground back into your body. If you're holding your breath, let yourself sigh and let go. If you're worried you might lose control if you let yourself go too much, set a timer and let yourself go for five or ten minutes. With your breath, let go of as much as you can without forcing or resisting—just be with yourself and breathe. There's no way to do it wrong.

Body Awareness

When we are feeling anxious, our body tends to tighten. In the mirror, you can see this tension. Look for it: tension around your eyes and jaw, a furrowed brow, hunched shoulders, clenched fist, grasping hands, and nervous gestures like biting your nails, scratching, and fidgeting. Get to know your habits by simply watching and being curious. Don't try to change them immediately. Just be open to getting to know your habits in the mirror. Choose one body part that seems to be calling for your attention and focus your attention on loosening and relaxing that part by sending your breath there. Notice any feelings that come up as you attempt to relax. Anxiety creates a sense of readiness in the body to warn off threats. If you purposely let go, you may find it brings up feelings of fear or vulnerability. You can't force yourself to relax. Be curious and listen to your body. Remember to see yourself with a kind intention.

Mental Focus

You may want to revisit the self-talk exercises in part 3. When you're feeling anxious, you can experiment with making video journals that describe how you feel. Experiment with self-talk in the different points of view: I feel anxious; you feel anxious; Tara feels anxious. Taking a broader perspective in the third person can calm you and help you find more compassion for yourself. Glance into your own eyes with kindness, from the second-person perspective, as though you were looking at a friend; this may help calm you too.

- - - **try this** - - -

Consider making a video for yourself to watch later when you're anxious. Pick a day and time when you are feeling good, optimistic, and relaxed. Access your inner nurturer and make a five- to ten-minute video to reassure and calm yourself to watch later when you're in an anxious state. By making this video, you'll be reminded that you are not in a constant state of anxiety, as may seem to be the case when you're feeling anxious. Remember to watch the video when you're feeling anxious.

32. How to Unfreeze Yourself

The fight-flight-freeze response is your body's natural reaction to danger. It's a response to stress that helps you react to perceived threats, like an oncoming car or growling dog. This response instantly creates hormonal and physiological changes. These changes allow you to act quickly so you can protect yourself. It's a primary instinct that our ancient ancestors developed for survival. Specifically, fight-or-flight is an active defense response where you stay and fight or quickly flee the scene. As a result, your heart rate gets faster, which increases oxygen flow to your major muscles. In addition, your pain perception drops, and your vision and hearing sharpen. These changes help you size up the situation accurately and respond rapidly.

Fight-flight-freeze isn't a conscious decision. It's an automatic reaction, so you can't control it in the moment. But over time, we can develop habits of responding to stress and managing our anxiety about real and, more often, imagined threats. We use adaptions of fight-flight-freeze to manage everyday anxieties, but they are usually not effective because most everyday challenges don't threaten our survival. You can use self-reflection to get out of these uncomfortable states so you can respond more effectively and with greater confidence and self-compassion. Let's take a look at each of these, beginning with freezing.

Freezing is fight-or-flight on hold. You become immobilized and stay entirely still, unable to fight or flee. Freezing can be a momentary "deer in the headlights" kind of experience. It can also show up when you feel public self-consciousness, like freezing when suddenly confronted by someone to answer a question. Whether it's from your boss in a meeting, your professor in the classroom, or a catcaller on the street, abruptly being put on the spot can make you freeze.

As discussed earlier, the best way to deal with anxiety and related reactions like freezing is to do deep breathing and ground into your body. In freezing, you hold your breath to remain entirely still. This can make you more anxious and maintain your immobilized state. Your body is also, well, frozen. So move it, stomp your feet, slap your thighs, get up, and move.

When we freeze, particularly in social situations, we lose the ability to speak up for ourselves. Sometimes, in the moment, being silent can be your best option. But if you find yourself freezing up at work, school, or social situations when you'd prefer to speak up, it's time for some uncensored mirror talk! What did you really want to say to your boss, your professor, that catcaller? Practice in front of the mirror or make video journals of what you want to say. By regularly practicing speaking up for yourself, you'll build confidence and be ready next time.

In her book, *Unbound: A Woman's Guide to Power*, Kasia Urbaniak teaches the art of verbal self-defense with particular attention to "the freeze" that many women experience when being put on the spot. In the case of the catcaller, you're walking down the street, and someone randomly yells, "Hey, nice [insert body part]!" You immediately freeze, like a frightened piece of prey, unable to move. Later you may feel self-reproach: How could you let a complete stranger do that to you? But, first, remember that it's an automatic conditioned response—you did not choose it.

Kasia suggests that if you're in a situation where you're made to feel uncomfortably self-conscious, try shifting your attention onto the person who's making you feel that way. For example, if someone says, "You look so pretty today—oh, now you seem kinda nervous." Don't say: "Why do you think so?" or "Screw you!" Instead, put the attention back on them by saying, "Where did you get that shirt?" or "Why are you standing there looking at me?" Anything to put the attention back on them and leave them feeling off-kilter instead of you.

We talked about the effects of inward- and outward-focused attention in part 1. To get out of the freeze, focus your attention outward as you breathe deeply and move your body. Ask a question back to give yourself time and space; simply, "Why do you ask that?" can break the freeze. Practice, practice, practice in front of the mirror so this response becomes your automatic response when you're put on the spot.

For instance, Becca felt herself freeze whenever her boss commented on her appearance. Her boss figured he was just being friendly and making small talk. He thought it was cute that Becca got all flustered and tongue-tied. But Becca felt helpless and humiliated because she couldn't stop herself from freezing up. It also took her a bit of time to recover from these intrusions and get back to her work.

I suggested that she do some mirror talk. In the first phase of her mirror talk, Becca let loose and said everything she wanted to tell her boss. Her dialogue was full of expletives. I encouraged her to keep going until she had said everything out loud that she'd wished she could say to her boss but froze and suppressed to keep her job.

Once she felt a sense of completion and exhaustion with that phase, we worked on short phrases that she could say to her boss to prevent the freeze in the moment. For instance, if her boss said, "I like your dress." Becca could say. "That's a nice shirt. Where did you get it?" Turning the attention off herself and back onto him. She practiced this in front of the mirror for what seemed to her like a million times. But it paid off. The next time her boss commented on her blouse, she turned the tables with, "That's a nice shirt. Where did you get it?" He replied, "My daughter gave it to me for my birthday." Bingo. Now Becca had a small talk topic that didn't make her freeze. Becca started to ask her boss about his daughter. This satisfied his desire for small talk and put her more at ease.

Have you ever wondered what you might look like when you freeze up?

Sabina Grasso is a photographer who suffered from anxiety attacks that would leave her frozen for hours. She once spent half a day sitting on the stairs of a train station, unable to move. She began to take self-portraits during her attacks and was eventually able to overcome her condition. Seeing herself in that helpless state gave her the self-awareness and the self-compassion she needed to gain control. We often instinctively avoid seeing ourselves in vulnerable and uncomfortable states. But letting ourselves see it from an observer perspective can initiate a powerful shift needed to change and heal. Maybe we should start a healing selfie movement!

33. Taking Flight and Coming Back from Dissociation

Have you ever caught a glimpse of yourself in the mirror and done a double take? Your first reaction is something like, "Who is that?" then you quickly realize it's you. This common experience is much more likely to occur when we are under stress. There's a temporary disconnection between our physical image and our feelings, thoughts, and body sensations.

But some people suffer from mental disorders in which they lose their ability to recognize themselves in the mirror altogether. These are classified as disassociation and depersonalization disorders by the American Psychological Association. People suffering from these disorders may avoid looking in the mirror because their own reflection is so foreign that it frightens them. How does this happen? When humans get too stressed out, the limbic part of the brain temporarily shuts down. The limbic system is responsible for awareness, experiencing reality, and making connections between people, places, and things. When this part of the brain shuts down, it dissociates from itself—in other words, it abandons itself. People with these disorders often have a history of trauma and emotional and physical abuse. In an attempt to escape from these painful experiences, they disconnected from themselves so frequently that they lost the ability to experience their feelings, thoughts, and body sensations. So now they don't recognize themselves in the mirror and often experience themselves as not even being real.

Most of us do milder versions of dissociation on occasion. For example, if you've ever spaced-out in the middle of a conversation, forgot why you walked into a room, or found your mind a million miles away during meditation, then you've momentarily left yourself. Some people develop the habit of dissociating or fleeing from stressful experiences, making it harder for them to come back and connect deeply with themselves.

For instance, James had a habit of spacing-out. He came for mirror meditation instruction because he wanted to be more present with himself and others. When we first began working together, he'd look in the mirror and say, "I don't feel real." I said, "That's okay. Just stay with yourself and let me know if anything changes." It didn't change for many sessions. But James kept coming back. I realized he liked being with me because he could feel that I was real and I did not make any demands on him to be a certain way. One day I had the idea to ask him to do some self-talk. I suggested that he complete a sentence in the mirror from the three different perspectives:

"If I was real..."

"If you were real..."

"If James was real..."

During this process, James uncovered some harsh self-judgments and difficult emotions that he could avoid experiencing when he disconnected from himself. He traced the habit of spacing-out back to his childhood. He was frequently yelled at by his father. It was terrifying for him as a small boy. He couldn't escape physically, so he disconnected from his body because he could not deal with the extreme fear. Now feeling unreal had become a habit of avoiding anything that might be uncomfortable. He also avoided making some difficult life decisions by feeling unreal: his job and his relationship were both unfulfilling. As he began to feel more real, he felt the discomfort and had to confront those facts. I encouraged him to stay with it and stay with himself. Once he made the connection and understood why and when he dissociated from himself, he had a choice to relate to himself and challenging situations differently. By doing his mirror meditation and video journaling regularly, he learned to tame his self-judgments, shift out of feeling threatened, and stay with himself when uncomfortable feelings arose.

34. Letting Go of the Fight to Heal the Heart

Fighting as a response to stress can take many forms. Let's consider how we can fight against ourselves when we are in the throes of great life changes. It can feel like we are pressing the accelerator and the brake at the same time. We end up creating more stress and pain through our resistance, and we end up getting nowhere.

Brenda, a lovely woman in her fifties, had a frozen shoulder, a muscular condition in which one's range of motion of the arm and shoulder is severely restricted. It usually doesn't have a direct physical cause, but it's often linked to emotions. Brenda had recently dealt with her mother's death and an abrupt ending to a long-term romantic relationship. She was anxious, restless, and very impatient with herself. She wanted to start a new business and get on with her life but complained, "This damn shoulder is slowing me down!" She was also having chest pain, which luckily turned out to be just more muscle tension. Her muscles seemed to be involuntarily resisting as if she were fighting against some hidden obstacle. She felt like she was spinning her wheels and not getting anywhere.

I asked her to sit in front of the mirror. After some centering and relaxation exercises, I suggested that she move her arms in whatever way she felt like moving. She immediately covered her heart with her hands. She told me she slept that way. Day and night, she was protecting her heart—apparently so aggressively that she was actually injuring herself. Her frozen shoulder came about and was maintained by the conscious and unconscious shielding of her heart. She began to work with a physical therapist to release the muscles in her arms and shoulder. She also worked to process her anxiety and grief with a psychotherapist. I showed her how to use the mirror to understand the connection between her body and her emotions.

I suggested she sit with herself in front of the mirror, placing her hand on her heart, and just be with herself in this way. Not trying to force herself to be more open, but to just be with her heart. After doing this regularly, her tears began to well up, and she started to release her feelings of deep sorrow for the endings of her most precious relationships. However, she was shy about expressing her feelings in front of me. So I suggested she simply be with herself and her heart for twenty minutes every day in front of the mirror.

After a time, she discovered it was fun to play with her reflection. As a child, she had a fascination with ballet. She loved the way the ballerinas moved their arms in *Swan Lake*. So she started to emulate those gentle, angulating movements in the mirror. Her arms seemed to be expressing what she couldn't put into words. She watched her arms express opposing desires. Her arms moved to protect her heart from being hurt and to reach out to love another. Watching herself move her arms in these ways helped her integrate the opposing desires. Eventually, her tears melted the shielding around her heart. She realized her arms and hands were expressing love and the desire to touch another and hold them and be held. This realization was a breakthrough that led to a release of deep emotion.

- - - try this - - -

1. Think of times in your life when you felt like you were pushing against yourself—or something that wasn't moving—and causing you frustration. Talk about it in your video journal. Try to locate where in your body you feel the most resistance. Bring your breath there and listen to what your body may be trying to tell you as you watch yourself in the mirror.

2. Review your video journals focusing on your hand gestures and body movements. What patterns do you notice? For example, how do you use your hands to express your feelings? Experiment in front of the mirror with various hand gestures: How do your hands want to move? What story do they tell?

PART VI

A Safe Space to Explore Your Emotions

35. How Emotions Are Reflected

The most satisfying moments that we share with other people are often those in which we feel seen, heard, and reflected in the moment. How does this happen?

A complex orchestra of facial expressions and body movements are part of any great conversation. We have the innate ability to associate the movements and facial expressions we see in other people with our own feelings or sensations so that we often unconsciously mirror the movements and expressions of others when we are in face-to-face conversation, especially if we like them! This is called *social mimicry,* and it occurs naturally during face-to-face interactions. We automatically, and often unconsciously, mimic the emotional expressions of the person we are interacting with. In this way, we mirror each other. In the process, we feel seen and heard and validated as humans.

We even have *mirror neurons* that fire when we merely observe another person's emotional state. The same parts of our own neuronal network are activated as those involved in processing that state in the other person. So when you watch someone having an emotional experience, your brain lights up in the same way as if you were having the emotional experience yourself.

We first learn about our emotions through our early face-to-face contact. We discover that certain emotions create different reactions in others through their nonverbal feedback, like social mimicry. Over time we learn the social rules for displaying our feelings. We typically come to understand that we should hide certain emotions in public. These are the so-called "negative" emotions of fear, anger, and sadness. We may find that people tend to avoid reflecting us directly when we are expressing these emotions strongly. They may unconsciously mimic for a second or two and then look away.

When we become consciously aware of the emotion, we choose to respond based on our past experiences. If you see a child afraid, your natural reaction will be to protect them, not just stand there mimicking them. If someone is sad, we may offer a gesture of comfort instead of looking sad back at them and thereby doubling the sadness. When someone is angry, we may try to avoid looking directly at them or try to appease them depending on the circumstances. Directly reflecting negative or difficult emotions is often ill-advised because it can make us and others feel worse.

So we learn that it is not okay to show them and may have self-judgments about feeling them due to our early learning experiences. Yet, we need our emotions reflected to feel them, accept them, and integrate them into our experience. We need to get comfortable with ourselves, and all our feelings, not just those others want to share with us. Because you are human, you can experience the whole gamut of human emotions even if others find some of these emotions uncomfortable or unacceptable.

Through our social experiences, we may learn that even *having* negative emotions makes us unlovable and that if we feel bad, we must be bad. Following emotional display rules is an integral part of social functioning. Still, in doing so, we may become so good at hiding our genuine emotions that we lose touch with ourselves or believe we are impostors obliged to hide our true feelings and put on a pleasant face no matter what.

The mirror and your video journal create a private space for you to explore your emotions. You won't have to worry about being judged by others or having to deal with their reactions. You can create a safe space to be curious about your emotions. You don't need to try and change them or fix them—or even justify them. You can allow yourself to feel them.

In this section, you can try out exercises that are designed to help you explore your emotions. Stories of people who had challenges around accepting, expressing, and managing their emotions will show how using self-reflective tools can help process difficult emotions and build greater emotional resilience.

36. Social Display Rules

How good is your poker face?

We use our faces to express emotions. In social interactions, we use facial expressions to signal to others how we want the conversation to go. But our faces may not be reflecting our innermost feelings. So as you're developing a relationship with yourself in the mirror, you might become aware of the fact that your emotions aren't showing up on your face in real time.

Through socialization, we learn rules for displaying our emotions. This leads us to be intentional about the emotions we show rather than expressing them spontaneously. Following emotional-display rules is an essential part of social functioning. But in doing so, we may become so good at hiding our genuine emotions that we can start to lose contact with how we're actually feeling. Yet, sharing all our emotions with others can create problems and misunderstandings too. We have to deal with other people's reactions to our emotions.

Smiling is one of the most common ways we use social display rules to signal intentions to others in social interactions. Everyone knows how to fake a smile. We learn when to show and hide our genuine emotions from early face-to-face exchanges. Our parents instinctively want to shield us from negative social experiences. They reward emotional displays that will encourage and facilitate acceptance from others. So as children, we learn to behave in specific ways to receive social approval. Developing a *social smile* to hide unacceptable emotions is part of the socialization process.

The social smile is often activated automatically. We may not be fully aware of it. For instance, you might smile reflexively to put the brakes on showing irritation or anger at a rude comment made during a social gathering. Your social smile may be activated when you're nervous in public, as part of being in a state of public self-consciousness. We can also intentionally smile to pepper our communication, like smiling reassuringly at someone who appears suspicious of us or flashing a quick smile at an attractive stranger from across the room to signal it's okay to approach.

Our daily communications involve a complex mixture of authentic and fake smiles. We use the social smile to manage others' reactions to us. Social expectations around smiling differ by gender and culture. Women's faces are more often scrutinized, objectified, and judged on attractiveness and friendliness. Women are encouraged to smile more than men. Whether it be an image consultant or a stranger on the street, everyone seems free to advise women to smile more. The term "resting bitch face," most often attributed to women, refers to the expectation that even when women are relaxing and not directly engaging with others, they are supposed to be sporting a pleasant upturn of the lips. If not, they're bitches!

How do you know whether an emotion is genuine?

Research finds that observers rely primarily on the eye and mouth regions to recognize emotions successfully.[46] Different emotions are most easily detected in different areas of the face. When the whole face is visible, we focus on the eyes to spot sadness and fear, whereas disgust and happiness are more reliably detected by concentrating on the mouth area. These two parts of the face can work in isolation or complex coordination.

Research finds that genuine emotion is particularly difficult to conceal in the eyes.[47] Still, micro-expressions in the eyes can be concealed by mouth movements. When we encounter someone we dislike, we may momentarily display a reflexive expression of disgust, only to follow up with a forced smile and greeting. Researchers wanted to know if these fake expressions were effective at hiding genuine emotions. They found that follow-up mouth movements can successfully conceal brief emotional changes in the eyes or micro-expressions thought to reflect real emotions.

Genuine smiles show in the eyes. Researchers of facial expression have consistently found distinct differences between obligatory social smiles and the authentic smile that naturally occurs when experiencing happiness or joy. The social smile is activated in the mouth muscles only. But a genuine smile, known as the Duchenne smile, named after the French anatomist who discovered it, involves both the mouth and the eyes. Interestingly, the facial muscle engaged by a genuine smile, called the orbicularis oculi, can't be activated on command. You can see an authentic smile in the crinkles around the eyes.

So, our facial expressions of emotion are both voluntary and involuntary. Genuine expressions happen automatically and reflect our internal emotional states, like smiling when you're feeling happy. But we can also consciously change our expressions to match cultural and social expectations.

- - - **try this** - - -

Often when people first start to do mirror meditation, they'll reflectively smile at themselves. There's nothing inherently wrong with this. But I invite you to be curious. Is it a social smile? A gesture designed to put you and others at ease? Something to do with your face to avoid the discomfort of not knowing what else to do? Or is it a genuine smile of recognition, love, and respect that you have for yourself?

Sit with yourself in front of the mirror for ten minutes with a completely neutral expression on your face, relax all your facial muscles, let them go slack, and see what happens. Then make a video journal to talk about your experience.

37. Discovering Your True Feelings

How many different emotions are there? The answer is up for debate. During the 1970s, psychologist Paul Ekman identified six basic emotions that he believed were evolutionary-based, therefore, experienced in all human cultures. The emotions he identified were happiness, sadness, disgust, fear, surprise, anger, and contempt. He and other researchers later expanded the list. Researchers found that these emotions are not entirely distinct. People experience them at different degrees of intensity. Also, different emotions blend, making unique emotions. And, no emotion is an island. Emotions are nuanced and complex, working together to create the rich and varied fabric of your emotional life.

For simplicity's sake, we will focus on the emotions that I have found to be particularly relevant to mirror meditation. I've worked with students and developed some techniques to help you manage fear, anger, sadness—and happiness.

It is also important to note that these exercises work with emotions in the range of intensity that's manageable for you. If you feel extremely unpleasant emotions that seem unmanageable, it's better to seek the help of a licensed therapist to help you process them. For example, together, we can work with irritation and mild anger. Still, if you're feeling rage or are concerned you might hurt yourself or others, please see a professional therapist right away. Likewise, if you experience intense, long-standing sadness, it may be classified as depression and you may need professional treatment. Chronic fear may be a symptom of post-traumatic stress and should be treated by a clinical psychologist.

We've already extensively discussed common everyday fear in the context of anxiety in part 5. So, here in part 6, we'll consider happiness, anger, and sadness. I've found anger to be the emotion we are most likely to hide from others, and maybe even ourselves. Anger can show up in many different forms in the mirror if we're willing to look. We've discussed anger and fear as blended as the fight component in the fight-flight-freeze response in the previous section. Here we consider other forms of anger, and later we'll discuss how anger can influence how we perceive others. But first, let's turn our attention to happiness.

Happiness

Of all the different emotions, happiness tends to be the one that people strive for the most. Happiness is often defined as a pleasant emotional state characterized by feelings of contentment, joy, gratification, satisfaction, and well-being. Happiness is expressed through facial expressions, like smiling, relaxed body posture, and an upbeat, pleasant tone of voice.

As a social function, expressing happiness plays an essential role in signaling friendliness and assuring that we are not a threat to others. Pleasant emotions like happiness motivate us to do things that are, by and large, good for us and the survival of our species (such as reproducing and child-rearing). The pursuit of happiness is often a primary motivation in our lives.

However, the concept of happiness can be pretty loaded. We receive lots of messages on what should make us happy. We might be judged on our ability to be happy. We may even get into competitions with others to prove we are happier than they are. Looking at happiness in the mirror, we may also have difficulty allowing ourselves to be happy. You may feel like you have to be constantly doing something to improve yourself. Maybe you got messages growing up that being too pleased with yourself was something that was frowned upon. Being too happy is a sign that something is wrong with you! Looking at yourself in the mirror when you are happy can bring up all kinds of self-judgments and other emotions. So the process can be quite illuminating. Experiencing true happiness with yourself in the mirror can be liberating.

Sadness

Sadness is an emotion that everyone experiences from time to time. It's our natural response to the loss of someone or something important. What causes sadness varies considerably based on personal and cultural notions of loss.

Sadness can take different forms, such as feelings of disappointment, grief, hopelessness, disinterest, and dampened mood. In some cases, people can experience prolonged and severe periods of sadness that can turn into depression. Sadness can be experienced in several ways, including crying, dampened mood, tiredness, quietness, and withdrawal from others.

The facial expression of sadness is easy to identify and hard to fake. One strong and reliable sign of sadness is the angling-up of the inner corners of the eyebrows. Few people can voluntarily manipulate these muscles, making it especially difficult to fake (unlike other facial movements).

The universal function of sadness is to signal for help. A sad facial expression can signal to others that we need comforting or to take some time and recoup from our loss. But, it can be challenging to ask for help when you feel sad due to social rules around expressing emotion. It's also tricky to know what to do when you recognize someone is feeling sad. For instance, if they are grieving the loss of a loved one, it's hard to know whether to express your sympathy and concern directly or try to distract them with other topics of conversation. Either way, you risk looking awkward and maybe even insensitive. So pretending we don't notice someone is sad can be an easy way out. Ironically, this type of polite social avoidance may contribute to people feeling even more lonely when sad about a loss. This is why it's so important to normalize sadness and to face it in yourself in the mirror. Often we avoid the feeling of sadness because we fear it may overwhelm us, but accepting and even embracing this emotion can be quite empowering.

Some people get pleasure from feeling sadness and may even seek out experiences that evoke sadness. Other people may have an extreme aversion to sadness and may go to great lengths to avoid situations that they believe may trigger the emotion. This may even cause some to avoid attachment or commitment since it could leave them vulnerable to loss and sadness; we'll discuss this more in part 8.

Anger

Anger is a very powerful emotion. It can show up as feelings of hostility, agitation, frustration, and antagonism toward others. Like fear, anger can play a part in your body's fight-or-flight response. When a threat generates feelings of anger, you may be inclined to fend off the danger and protect yourself.

Anger is often displayed through facial expressions, such as frowning or glaring, taking a strong stance or turning away, and a harsh tone of voice. Anger shows up on your face as eyebrows coming down and together, glaring eyes, and narrowing the corners of the lips. If you consciously suppress anger (or have unconscious repression of anger), the expression will be less obvious, though it may show a flash of anger in a split-second micro-expression.

The typical sensations of anger include feeling hot (like the term "seeing red"), sweating, muscle tension, and clenching one's jaw and fists. You may find yourself leaning forward with your head or chin jutting forward and puffing your chest or body to appear larger.

While anger is often thought of as a negative emotion, it can sometimes be a good thing. It can be constructive in helping clarify your needs in a relationship, and it can also motivate you to take action and find solutions to things that are bothering you.

However, anger can become a problem when it is excessive or expressed in ways that are unhealthy, dangerous, or harmful to others. Uncontrolled anger can quickly turn to aggression, abuse, or violence. Unchecked anger can make it difficult to make rational decisions and can even impact your physical health. So we must learn how to manage it well.

As with sadness, it is often easier to avoid someone who is angry than face them directly. So, many people aren't comfortable with seeing their own anger or seeing the anger of others. Mirror meditation can help you get to know your anger and work with it constructively.

Emotions play a critical role in how we live our lives, from influencing how we engage with others in our day-to-day lives to affecting our decisions. By understanding some of the different types of emotions, you can understand how these emotions are expressed and the impact they have on your behavior.

- - - try this - - -

You've probably developed beliefs around having and expressing certain emotions. You can explore these by doing the following sentence-completion exercises in your video journal—experiment with using the three different points of view. Do the exercise for each emotion several times until you feel you've exhausted all your possible responses. Then look back on your video from a centered, open, compassionate place and see what you discover.

When I am happy, I...

When you are angry, you...

When Tara is sad, she...

Consider the difference between *having* an emotion and *being* in the state of an emotion.

If I have too much happiness, I...

If I have too little happiness, I...

If you have too much anger, you...

If you have too little anger, you...

If Tara has too much sadness, Tara...

If Tara has too little sadness, Tara...

38. Emotional Labor and Authenticity

When I was a waitress in college, I learned to recite the ingredients in the house salad for my customers. I must have said it over a million times. In fact, many years later, I still remember exactly what I said, oh so cheerfully, "A mixed-green salad, tossed in a creamy Caesar-based dressing, garnished with blue cheese and bacon bits." "Sure, I'd be happy to put that on the side for you!!" with a big smile.

There is often a strong expectation of being cheery and positive to create good feelings in business and social interactions. When we actually don't feel that way, it creates a strain or a burden, called emotional labor.

The dictionary says emotional labor is the process of managing feelings and expressions to fulfill the emotional requirements of a job. More specifically, you are expected to regulate your emotions during interactions with customers, coworkers, and managers. This includes expressing emotions that you don't actually feel, like enthusiasm when hearing about a new project you've been assigned or regret when a customer complains about something that wasn't your fault. Emotional labor also involves suppressing your true feelings, like anger when a customer insults you or glee when a dishonest coworker gets caught. This is all done, consciously and strategically, to create positive feelings in the customers or clients so the business can succeed—and so you can keep your job!

Emotional labor can also pertain to the emotional burdens of family members, partners in a relationship, and those responsible for childcare. Women are often assigned the role of emotional labor. It is their job to monitor the feelings of others and act in ways to promote good feelings in everyone else, regardless of how they are actually feeling.

Jobs involving emotional labor often are defined as those that require face-to-face or voice-to-voice contact with the public and the expectation that the worker produce an emotional state in another person, for instance, a happy, satisfied customer.

You can perform emotional labor in two different ways: surface acting and deep acting.

Surface acting is when employees display the emotions required for a job without changing how they actually feel. For instance, I actually wasn't thrilled to fetch house salads in my waitress role all night long, yet I smiled to make my customers feel welcome and cared for.

Deep acting is a more effortful process in which employees change their internal feelings to align with organizational expectations, producing more natural and genuine emotional displays. For instance, if you are going through a difficult personal challenge, you may feel distressed. You can take a few minutes to put your personal feelings aside and remember the purpose of your job, why you like it, what your responsibilities entail, and how you contribute positively to the lives of others. Then you act from that place inside you.

Both surface and deep acting are designed to reach the same end: happy customers and positive bottom-line outcomes. However, research has shown surface acting is more harmful to employee health.[48] Generally, acting in ways inconsistent with how you are actually feeling regularly can negatively impact your physical and mental health. So what can you do instead?

First, pick a job that you enjoy and that is consistent with your values. If that is not possible, try some deep acting in the mirror. Breathe, ground into your body, and use self-talk to create a set of affirmations to remind you of your greater purpose. Also, make sure you have a healthy outlet for your true feelings.

Clara worked in the service industry. She heard my waitress story and really identified with it. She needed her waitressing job to cover college expenses. Clara hated it, but she knew it wouldn't last forever. She was starting to feel numb and irritable. Clara came for mirror meditation instruction to get some support. I suggested that before she dove into deep acting that she explore her true feelings through video journaling. Every night after her shift ended, I told her to make a ten-minute video just expressing anything on her mind or in her heart. This turned out to be a very powerful exercise for her. She did not realize how deeply some of her customers' comments were affecting her—or how much of a strain it was to smile all night long. At the end of the night, her cheeks actually hurt. Clare hadn't even noticed it before. She often talked for longer than ten minutes, some-times just ranting to release all the pent-up emotions she'd been suppress-ing all night. By watching her videos later from a calm, centered place, Clara felt compassion for herself and appreciation for how hard she was trying to do a good job. Eventually, she even found humor in some of the kooky interactions with customers. Her videos gave her a broader perspec-tive. She learned to take it all a bit more lightly.

39. Facing Anger

I was acquainted with Katherine as a colleague for many years. At an event where I gave a talk and did a mirror meditation demonstration, she came up to me afterward. She remarked how angry she looked and that she had not seen that side of herself before.

Katherine had a somewhat harsh, aggressive demeanor, so she was perhaps the last to know how she came across to others. Basically, everyone of afraid of her. With her a furrowed brow, tight mouth, and sharp piercing eyes, she seemed, and looked, mean.

"My husband and kids are always telling me I look mean. Do you think I look mean?" Yikes! Luckily, I know a million ways that a mirror can save the day. So I simply replied, "What does it look like to you in the mirror?" "I can help you decide for yourself." I offered.

When she came for mirror meditation instruction, I asked her about her experience with anger and meanness. She told me that she'd had angry outbursts all her life. She just couldn't seem to control her temper. As a child, her parents would quickly back off or do whatever it took to appease her. Katherine was supersmart in school, and because she performed so well and was female, she was never labeled as a child with behavior problems.

Katherine married Will, who was a super intelligent and agreeable guy. He took great pride in his ability to handle difficult people, especially women. So he saw Katherine as a challenge; he thought she was exciting, and he liked being needed by her. Will typically smoothed over the many disputes and ruffled feathers caused by Katherine's abruptness. He found her occasional outbursts charming; they added a touch of drama to everyone's experience. In Katherine's mind, she was simply honest and authentic with people. She didn't want to waste their time or hers with unnecessary niceties. And what was the harm in stirring things up on occasion?

Something shifted when she did her first mirror meditation, so she came to find out more. She remarked, "I looked furious! I almost scared myself!" She chuckled. Then turning serious. "I want to know why." As we've discussed in part 3, asking why things happen as they do is not all that helpful when we are trying to change. I did not want to go down a why rabbit hole with Katherine. I'm sure we could find many things in her life and the world, in general, to be angry about. I wanted to focus on what to do now. How would she like to feel? How would she like her face to look to her husband and kids?

But first, she had to get comfortable with seeing her anger for herself.

As she sat in front of the mirror, her agitation rose. She seemed to want to push the experience along instead of being in the moment and letting things unfold. I advised her to practice sitting in front of the mirror for five minutes and then work up to ten, fifteen, and twenty minutes per day. She needed to do her mirror meditation on her own without interruptions. She had been relying on others to smooth things over when she got frustrated. Her anger also enlivened her to make hurtful comments to others.

Generally speaking, anger can easily cause harm to ourselves and others. Psychologists are unclear about whether the wish to harm is built into the core of anger or something we learn, but we know it is often a part of the anger process that gets us into trouble. By looking at herself when she felt the desire to make a hurtful comment, she was able to break the cycle.

She worked with a psychotherapist who specialized in anger management. Mindful mirror meditation helped her strengthen her ability to decide how to react to something—as it was not the anger itself but its expression that often got her into trouble.

Katherine created a space in her house to do mirror meditation every day. She was not to be disturbed. In the process, she came to know her anger intimately and naturally discovered many of the whys without going on a big mental tangent. She realized she often got angry when she needed space and was feeling overwhelmed. Under her anger were often more vulnerable and helpless feelings. She got whipped up into a rage, felt helpless, and didn't trust anyone to help her. She sensed everyone was backing away and afraid of her, which increased her rage, underneath which lived a deep sense of panic and sense of helplessness. Katherine created a safe space for herself to see this pattern in the mirror. Just letting herself cry and freak-out in front of the mirror was healing for her. Together with her therapist, she worked to change the pattern. When she started to feel a tinge of irritation, she paid attention to it, listened, and looked to the feeling underneath the surface.

As a side note, you may have heard about catharsis as a treatment for bottled-up anger. The idea is that you designate an object to represent a person that you're (still) angry with, be it a parent, sibling, former boss, or partner. You imagine that person is, say, a pillow, and then you beat the crap out of it. In theory, you're safely releasing your bottled-up anger onto a pillow in your therapist's office. However, research shows that cathartic techniques actually make people *angrier*.[49] Facing your anger and the vulnerable feelings it is protecting is a better strategy, though not an easy one. Find a therapist who specializes in anger management who'd be willing to support you in doing a deep exploration. It's likely to be worth it!

40. Facing Sadness

Amber's parents read psychology books that instructed them to reward the desired behaviors in their children by giving their children attention and to discourage undesirable behaviors by withdrawing their attention. In theory, Amber would learn how to behave through rewards and punishments. Amber's parents weren't very comfortable with their own emotions and had a strong desire for Amber to be a happy little girl. So when Amber smiled and giggled, her parents showered her with attention and praise. When Amber got upset, cried, frowned, and was fussy, her parents withdrew their attention until Amber returned to her happy smiling self again.

As a child, Amber learned what to do to get her parents' attention. As she grew older, Amber found that being happy and smiling attracted more exciting people and opportunities. The only problem was Amber was human, so she felt the full range of human emotions, or at least she did when she was young. These days she wasn't sure how she felt about anything. Amber just knew she was exhausted and alone. She came for mirror meditation instruction because she wanted to be more authentic in how she related to others. She was tired of putting on her happy-go-lucky persona and these days found herself spending more and more time alone thinking about the past.

Her first impulse was, of course, to smile at herself in the mirror. I suggested she relax her face, let all the muscles in her face go slack. "I feel nothing. I can't do this," she said. I assured her she could do mirror meditation without feeling anything. This is probably exactly what she needed to do to start her practice. I suggested that she take twenty minutes a day and just sit with herself in front of the mirror with no goal other than to be with herself for twenty minutes.

Amber had had enough psychotherapy to understand that her upbringing influenced her as an adult. But facing herself in the mirror took her to a deeper level of self-awareness. She discovered some pretty intense self-judgments about feeling nothing. She realized she was still very much under the control of her early childhood training to keep smiling to prevent herself from becoming invisible to others. She believed to her core that she somehow had to be in a fabulous mood at all times or else she wouldn't be liked or accepted or worthy of attention. Looking in the mirror intensified the power of those early messages about being seen as only happy and pleasant.

Amber did mirror meditation sessions in conjunction with her psychotherapy. Amber discovered that she had so little support when she was distressed as a child that she just went numb as an adult. She had no way to process her feelings. It was as if she became invisible to herself.

She learned that having negative emotions led people to leave her. In the process, she lost her connection to her parents, and she lost contact with herself too. She established an emotional connection with her therapist, who accepted and welcomed all of Amber's emotions, and the mirror helped her establish this connection with herself.

As she became more committed to her personal growth, an overwhelming feeling of sadness came. She felt the loss of her parents' love and how she withdrew from relationships with friends because she did not feel she could maintain them because people would eventually find out what a terribly unhappy person she really was. She needed to grieve the loss of these opportunities and accept her past decisions. She did not feel good enough or happy enough to make commitments to others. Amber thought she needed to be in a happy mood always, and she knew she just couldn't do it any longer, so she stopped trying.

Now sitting with herself in front of the mirror, the sadness felt like she was falling into a black hole. Once she started crying, Amber thought she would never stop and just fall deeper and deeper into a pit of grief. Her therapist helped her remember that she was essentially abandoned by her parents when she was in distress as a child. She learned that it was dangerous to be distressed and that no one would be there for her if she needed help. Unlearning that took time. She needed to practice letting others support her. And, learning to support herself through mirror meditation was key to the healing process.

PART VII

What Narcissus Can Teach You

41. Reflecting on Narcissus

When I first started working on this mirror meditation project, I'd go to social gatherings in Manhattan where there were many people from wellness and meditation communities. I'd tell them I was using mirrors as a meditation tool. On more than one occasion, eyes would flash with indignation, "That's narcissism!" Yet, for every criticism I'd encounter, there was an email or a comment, "Hey, I tried that mirror meditation. Wow it's really powerful. Thank you."

Deep down I knew the project was worthwhile because I saw how much it was helping people. Yet, I was feeling a gnawing sense of doubt. Is looking at yourself in the mirror really narcissistic? By now, I hope I've convinced you it's not. After doing a fair amount of investigation into the link between mirrors and narcissism, I've discovered some reasons why we may have complex feelings about our self-image and why the word "narcissism" can be so emotionally charged.

Perhaps you've seen classic paintings of Narcissus gazing at his reflection in a clear watery pool, completely in love with himself. In this section, I share insights into the link between mirror gazing and narcissism. You'll find there is much to learn from this association. What narcissists are trying to find in the mirror is deeply human, not an aberration. Lack of empathy and compassion are cornerstones of narcissism. By understanding how these deficits came about, we can better understand ourselves and develop empathy and compassion for others, including narcissists.

"Narcissist" is a word that gets used a lot. In fact, if you google it, you'll get over sixty million results. To say we have a casual interest in the topic is an understatement!

What is narcissism exactly? The dictionary defines it as an excessive interest in or admiration of oneself and one's physical appearance. But when people say, "Oh that person is a narcissist," they are usually referring to some variant of the symptoms of narcissistic personality disorder. To be diagnosed the NPD, you must display at least five of the following symptoms:

- a grandiose sense of self-importance, for example, exaggerating achievements and talents, expecting to be recognized as superior without commensurate achievements

- a preoccupation with fantasies of unlimited success, power, brilliance, beauty, or ideal love

- a belief that you are "special" and unique and can only be understood by, or should associate with, other special or high-status people

- a need for excessive admiration

- a sense of entitlement, as in unreasonable expectations of especially favorable treatment or automatic compliance with your expectations

- being interpersonally exploitative, as in taking advantage of others to achieve your own ends

- a lack of empathy or an unwillingness to recognize or identify with the feelings and needs of others

- being frequently envious of others or believing that others are envious of you

- showing arrogant, haughty behaviors or attitudes

You are probably very familiar with the narcissistic character pattern that plays out in fiction, reality shows, and real life: grandiosity with expectations of superior treatment, bullying, manipulating and exploiting others, a sense of entitlement, and an intense need for admiration. Though only 1 percent of the population fits the criteria to be diagnosed with full-blown narcissistic personality disorder,[50] we commonly see milder versions on the spectrum.

The critical feature of narcissism is a lack of empathy. We learn empathy skills through face-to-face contact. So it's an interesting coincidence that narcissists seem to love looking at their own image in the mirror but can't see others very well.

Why are we fascinated by narcissists? And what can we learn about ourselves from them? There is a unique and intimate connection between narcissism and mirrors. And our profound interest in this beguiling character is no accident. It's linked to our deep need for love and acceptance for who we truly are—and for accurate reflection. This need often goes unfulfilled for many of us. It's a common disappointment that we may be sharing without even realizing it.

We've discussed the importance of reflection in our formative years. While growing up, most everyone had experiences in which they weren't reflected accurately. The frequency, degree, and intensity of those experiences and how they are balanced with other experiences affects how our personality takes shape. Many factors can contribute to promoting the development of narcissistic tendencies. Most of these have to do with parents (and others) not giving children realistic reflection. Parents give excessive admiration, but it's not balanced with realistic criticism of the child. Or they may dole out lavish praise for good behaviors and excessive criticism for bad behaviors. The child may come to believe they are so powerful because their behavior creates such strong reactions in others. The child may be overindulged or excessively praised by adults for perceived exceptional physical appearance or abilities. The children who develop narcissistic tendencies may also experience unpredictable or unreliable caregiving, emotional abuse, or psychological manipulation. Any combination of these factors can become a recipe for narcissism. As a result, the child grows into an adult who doesn't have a realistic sense of who they are. In essence, they don't understand their real strengths and vulnerabilities, nor do they have accurate insight into how their behavior affects others.

Psychologists have observed a general rise in narcissistic tendencies in adults and children too. One factor has been the prevalence of self-esteem programs that advocate having a high degree self-confidence that is based more on image than experience. You can practice only focusing on the positive aspects of yourself and ignore any shortcomings. The problem is, boosting self-worth through positive affirmations and slogans, flattering selfie apps, and the like bypasses the experiences needed to develop emotional resilience and true confidence. Research shows that you can't protect your self-esteem by shielding yourself from failure. In fact, it's quite the opposite. To develop a realistic sense of confidence and esteem, you must fully experience both successes and failures, triumphs and disappointments too.

- - - **try this** - - -

1. Consider the ways in which you were reflected accurately and not so accurately by others in your life. Make some five- to ten-minute video journals describing these experiences. Was there a parent or teacher whom you felt really saw you accurately? What was the experience like? How did it impact you?

2. Then recall some individuals who simply didn't see you accurately. How did that feel? Experiment with telling the stories in the first person, second person, and third person and see how that might give you different insights.

3. Reflect on your attitudes and feelings about narcissism. Do you know someone who you think is a narcissist? What is it about them that leads you to believe they are narcissistic? How would you like to see them change in how they relate to you?

42. Empathy: Feeling What You Feel

The hallmark of the narcissism is lack of empathy and compassion for others. Without these, we can get stuck in a loop of self-absorption that cuts off opportunities to build satisfying, intimate relationships. By understanding how empathy and compassion develop, we can uncover some important clues about our own needs and why it's so frustrating when people we love don't see us with empathy and compassion.

The words "empathy" and "compassion" are often used interchangeably, but it's important to understand the distinction. Empathy is an automatic emotional response and resonance. When you see the grimace of pain on someone's face, your own face will grimace as though you're experiencing that pain too. If you're highly empathic, you'll tend to easily feel what others are feeling. Compassion is more of a cognitive perspective-taking, which we'll discuss in detail in the next chapter.

Empathy involves the ability to resonate with the emotions felt by others. We have the innate ability to associate the movements and facial expressions we see in other people with our own feelings or sensations. In fact, we often unconsciously imitate the same movements or expressions that we experience in others. For instance, in a conversation, particularly with someone you like or are familiar with, you'll tend to modulate your voices in synchrony. Two speakers' voices start out with distinct vocal patterns and by the end of the conversation, particularly if it's going well, their intonations, cadence, and volume will be similar. The conversation weaves together like a melody.

Another basis for empathy is social mimicry in face-to-face conversation. This is the phenomenon that occurs naturally during most interactions, in which we automatically, and often unconsciously, mimic the emotional expressions of the person we are interacting with. When we "sync up" with them as both our voices modulate and resonate, we begin imitating each other's movements. This automatic process creates a mirroring effect. Our *mirror neurons* fire when we merely observe another person's emotional state. The same parts of our own neuronal network are activated as the ones involved in processing that state in the other person. So when you watch someone having an emotional experience, your brain lights up in the same way as if you were having the emotional experience yourself.

It's clear that we're wired for emotional resonance with each other. But, there can be great variability in one's capacity to experience empathy. The capacity for empathy is shaped by our early experiences. At the most basic level, we learn empathy through repeated face-to-face interactions with others. Parenting plays a vital role in the development of empathy. Children learn empathy through repeated, face-to-face interactions in real time. Not surprisingly, empathic parents tend to have empathic children. But even if you didn't have perfectly empathic parents, you can improve your empathy skills. When you're more empathic, you'll get better at knowing your own feelings and those of others, which can help you improve your communication and bond with others.

Focusing your attention is essential for cultivating empathy. Make the time for face-to-face interactions with others, without your attention divided by multitasking and your devices. Research shows that babies prefer direct eye contact and those who imitate them.[51] It seems we're wired for face-to-face connection from birth. The need for attention is, in fact, quite essential to our survival. Infants can't sustain life unless others pay attention to them and respond to their needs—so we're hardwired to pull focus to us. A great example of this natural process is the fact that eye gazing between mother and infant releases oxytocin, which is a hormone that creates neural chemical changes in the brain that generate the euphoric feelings that promote bonding. We will explore eye gazing between adults in part 10.

In order to skillfully use your empathic ability, you must be able to tolerate your own emotions and not be overwhelmed by them. If you aren't able to tolerate your emotions, you may have difficulty tolerating the emotions of others. Early in life when we are just learning self-control, we have experiences with our caregivers that help us learn about our feelings. If your parent was able to attend to your emotions and empathically reflect them back to you, it probably helped you gain the ability to tolerate your feelings and stay in relationship with another person while you were feeling them. If your parent wasn't able to attend to your emotions, for whatever reason, then your feelings weren't recognized and you might not have learned how to tolerate them as well. In this case, you may feel like you only have yourself to rely on, and you can develop a habit of self-focus. Like anyone in pain, be it a toothache or a heartache, it's challenging to focus on anything but your pain. The exercises you did in parts 5 and 6 are designed to help you develop your emotional awareness and build tolerance for stronger emotions.

- - - try this - - -

1. Think about the people you've known throughout your life. Is there someone who stands out as particularly empathic? Share in your video journal what it felt like to be in the company of this person. How did you know they were being empathic, and what was its effect on you?

2. Reflect on a time when you wish there was a specific person (parent, partner, or friend) who would have lent an empathic ear. What about this experience did you find the most unsatisfying? What, specifically, were you longing for from them?

43. Compassion: Knowing What You Feel

Empathy often happens automatically. If you see someone grimace in pain, you grimace too. Then, as you discover more about the situation, you might start to respond compassionately.

Compassion is the ability to imagine yourself in someone else's shoes. For instance, if you hear of another's misfortune, you can imagine how you'd feel in that situation. You can do this deliberately. Compassion is essential to form meaningful relationships with others. Having a willingness and ability to understand how others feel and experience things differently from yourself allows you to connect deeply with others and sustain relationships over time.

Compassionate perspective-taking is a two-step cognitive process: first you must identify another's emotions as separate from your own, and then, you can draw on your skills to respond to them in a helpful way. To understand the emotional states of another person, you have to take on their perspective. You may then choose to respond in a similar way, such as feeling joy and delight when someone tells you of a success. Or you may react in a way that is not the same as the original emotional state of the other person, such as when the person is angry or upset, you may respond by being calm and attentive.

Compassion is learned. Your experiences growing up can have a profound impact on your ability to be compassionate. If your parents focused on your needs, they were essentially modeling how to understand and take the perspective of others. If your parents were focused only on their own needs, such as their desire to have a perfect child, a pretty child, a smart child, and so on, then you might not have had the experience of receiving compassionate understanding. So it will be more difficult to take that perspective with others. Instead, you may focus on others' expectations of you and how to act in ways that get attention and approval, or you may maintain an intense self-focus, which keeps people at a distance.

When your own emotional needs are satisfied, you can learn to understand the emotions and needs of others. Our compassion grows when we are with people who have developed compassion themselves. If your parents aren't comfortable with their feelings of vulnerability, they may not have been as tolerant of the vulnerable feelings in their children. People who can accept and express a wide range of emotions can model that capacity for others. If your parents allowed themselves to be seen frustrated, disorganized, and sad, in a sense, they gave you permission to be less than perfect yourself. But if your parents rejected their own negative emotions and only showed you a narrow range of "happy/nice" feelings and behaviors, then you might have come to believe that there was something wrong with you if you felt anything else.

When our needs are met early in life, it's easier to believe the world is a kind place, and the intention to be kind is our default perspective toward others.

Compassionate people seem to have a knack for taking another's point of view and being able to attend to their needs while staying aware of their own needs and feelings—and letting those be seen by others as well.

- - - **try this** - - -

Think about the people you've known throughout your life. Is there someone who stands out as particularly compassionate? Write or share in your video journal what it felt like to be in the company of this person. How did you know they were being compassionate, and what was its effect on you?

44. Why Compassion Might Be Better than Empathy

Naturally empathic people feel the pain of others acutely. So you may ask: Is it possible to be too empathic? Could feeling too deeply for someone else's pain or sorrow actually hurt you?

Too much empathy can be problematic. For one thing, when we become too distressed about the suffering of others, we don't have the cognitive and emotional resources available to do much to help them. Having compassion, a cognitive understanding of how they're feeling, is better for our own well-being and the well-being of those in need.

The idea that there can actually be too much empathy can be traced back to early Buddhist teachings. Instead of focusing on empathy to the point of draining ourselves emotionally, Buddhism teaches the practice of compassion, called *karuna*. This is the idea of sharing in suffering, having concern for another, but essentially feeling *for* and not feeling with the other.

Neuroscientists Tania Singer and Olga Klimecki conducted studies to compare the effects of empathy and compassion.[52] Two separate experiment groups were trained to practice either empathy or compassion. Their research revealed fascinating differences in the brain's reaction to the two types of training.

First, the empathy training activated the parts of the brain linked to emotion and self-awareness, and to emotion and consciousness, and also the area where pain is registered. The compassion group, however, stimulated activity in the areas connected to learning, decision making, and the reward system.

Second, the two types of training led to very different emotions and attitudes toward action. The empathy-trained group actually found empathy uncomfortable and troublesome. The compassion group, on the other hand, created positivity in the minds of the group members. The compassion group ended up feeling kinder and more eager to help others than those in the empathy group.

So by having a cognitive understanding of another's distress, rather than feeling it with them, you're in a better position both to help them and to take care of yourself.

Empathic distress comes about when we can't separate our own suffering from the suffering of others. It can lead to burnout and a variety of mental and physical health challenges. If emotions are running high and you find yourself getting swept away by the turmoil, here are some tips to avoid empathic distress.

First remember to breathe. When we see something distressing, it activates the fight-or-flight response, and our breathing becomes fast and shallow, which increases our anxiety and gives our emotions momentum. Research shows that slow, steady deep breathing activates the vagal nerve, which comes from the brain and controls the parasympathetic nervous system, which controls the relaxation response. A few deep breaths will help you feel calmer.

Second, feel your body. When you're witnessing strong emotions in others, intend to stay with yourself rather than getting caught up in their experience. Feel your feet on the ground and wiggle your toes. Bend your knees slightly if you are standing, and feel your butt in the chair supporting you if you're sitting. Be aware of body sensations and imagine yourself holding the sensations and emotions as they move through your body. And, of course, keep the option open to physically remove yourself from situations that become too distressing.

Third, glance in the mirror. When you're caught up in emotions, it's easy to forget yourself. Taking moment to look into your eyes can ground you back to reality, help you remember who you are, and put the immediate situation into a broader perspective. This is a time when your self-compassionate mirror meditation practice will come in handy.

Consider the following questions and record your thoughts and reactions in your video journal. Do you naturally feel empathy for others? Or do you tend to relate to others with compassionate understanding? Are there particular emotions that you find harder to empathize with than others? Do you ever wish there were less empathic feelings and more compassionate understanding in your communications? Does empathy ever get in the way of your compassionate understanding?

45. Compassion for the Narcissist

As we learned in the last chapter, whether or not a person takes compassionate action may have more to do with their ability to regulate their emotions than their moral character. So let's come back to our friend gazing at his reflection, unable to tear himself away to see anyone else. The hallmark of narcissism is the *lack* of empathy and compassion. Recent studies in neuroscience on the brains of narcissists point to some factors that may help you understand why some people have serious limitations on their capacity for empathy and compassion and how you might even be able to improve your own capacity for these vital interpersonal skills.

Many experiments and clinical observations find that narcissists have a habitual self-absorbed perspective that seems to prevent them from being aware of the emotions and experiences of others. But are they being rude and callous intentionally? Recent studies in neuroscience suggest that their lack of empathy and compassion may come from deficits in cognitive processing of emotion that aren't under their conscious control. These findings illuminate how we all can fall short of being as empathic and compassionate as we'd like to be. Let's take a closer look of what's happening in the brain of a narcissist.

Empathy involves sharing, imagining, and understanding the emotions of others. Neuroscience research has found that there are specific areas of the brain that activate when we experience empathy. One area of the brain is the anterior insula, which acts like a switch between two separate networks of cognitive processing: one is concerned with doing tasks, and other, called the default mode, is involved in self-focus. In other words, our brains can switch between focusing on a task or focusing on ourselves, but it's hard to do both simultaneously.

Recent brain imaging studies suggest that narcissists' deficit in empathy is due to a dysfunction in the anterior insula.[53] There seems to be an imbalance in which the anterior insula can't turn off the default mode network, which centers one's attention on the self. So, in other words, the brains of narcissists show that they can't stop thinking about themselves. Of course this might hinder one's ability to share and understand the emotions of others.

Other research suggests that narcissists might not be intentionally or willfully uncaring, but simply be less able to recognize and understand the emotions of others. Being able to recognize emotions via facial expressions is an important skill related to empathy.

In studies that used a classic test of recognizing and understanding facial expressions of fear, anger, disgust, joy, and sadness, narcissists showed deficits in emotion recognition, particularly for fear and anger.[54] This tendency for narcissists to perform worse in the recognition task held irrespective of how long they had to recognize the emotion. So, narcissists have difficulty recognizing distress (via fear and anger) in others, which would impede them from empathizing with others.

In the neuroimaging experiment, research participants who scored high and low on a narcissism test did a task that involved empathizing with pictures of emotional faces. Narcissists showed lower deactivation of the parts of the brain concerned with self-focus, again, suggesting narcissists had difficulty turning off their self-focus. On a questionnaire, the high narcissism group reported more self-oriented feelings of personal anxiety and unease in stressful interpersonal settings than those classified as low on narcissism. So, narcissists have difficulty controlling self-focus, recognizing others' emotions, and regulating their anxiety—and these appear to be the causes of their problems empathizing and responding compassionately.

So, if you accuse someone of being a selfish narcissist, you may be simply reinforcing their self-focus and contributing to their anxiety. Instead, see if you can get them to focus on you and be very explicit about expressing your feelings. Realize it might take them longer to grasp what you're feeling than you think. And, remember they may be grappling with more anxiety on the inside than is apparent from the outside. By staying calm, you'll make it easier for them to connect with you.

Of course, hard-core narcissists probably won't pick up on these cues. But I hope this research convinces you that many well-intentioned people might be too caught up and involved with themselves in the moment to show you their compassionate understanding. Maybe you can relate to this yourself. If you have ever felt like you've missed an opportunity to express compassion to someone who really needed it, you're not alone.

- - - try this - - -

1. Can you recall a time when you were very upset or annoyed and someone you care about wanted your attention and caring, and you were not able to give it to them? Write about this experience or make a video journal describing it and then review it later.

2. Notice your reaction to others who are expressing fear or anger. Is it harder to respond compassionately to them? See if you can break down your reaction next time someone you are close to expresses fear or anger. What is your immediate response? What gets in the way of your empathic or compassionate response?

46. Using the Mirror to Find What's Missing

How did narcissism become associated with the mirror anyway? In all of our meaningful relationships, we have a need to be seen, reflected, and appreciated by the other person. Early studies in psychoanalysis identified a particular kind of patient that seemed to have an extreme need to be seen, recognized, understood, related to, admired, and appreciated. In these case studies, analysts observed a pattern of relating to others that was similar to the story of Narcissus. Their patients had a "mirror transference" in which their relationships became a one-way reflection. They wanted the other person to see them as unique and special. And they expected others to be accurately attuned and empathic to them at all times, but could not do the same for the other person. Their need to be seen, attended to, and mirrored seemed insatiable.

Psychologists believe that mirror transference is a consequence of inadequate mirroring of one's essential nature in the formative years. We discussed the concept of basic goodness in part 3, and our inherent human nature is sometimes called one's core essence, unconditional goodness, or basic goodness. It's the part of ourselves that is pure and good. We don't have to do anything to earn it or cultivate it. This quality is simply who we are at our most fundamental humanness. Poets have described it as seeing the soul or light in a loved one's eyes. If this essential nature is not recognized and reflected when we are very young, we create an idealized self-image based on how we have been seen and reflected. Appearance, abilities, or accomplishments are usually the bases of this idealized self-image. Narcissists mistake who they really are for this idealized self and end up developing an insatiable need for reflection. They erroneously seek reflection for their looks, talents, or accomplishments. This type of reflection is never truly satisfying because what they crave is the reflection of their essential nature.

From the narcissist's perspective, therapists, significant others, friends and coworkers, fans, and followers are all there to serve one primary function: to mirror back their greatness. Narcissists see others as mirrors for themselves. Others are not seen as separate individuals with complex thoughts and feelings of their own. Narcissists use others for idealized reflection of themselves. This insatiable need for recognition, praise, and accolades (called narcissistic supply) keeps the narcissist from feeling the pain and vulnerability of not being seen for who he truly is. So, the mirror itself is merely a tool for self-admiration.

The theme of equating self-worth with physical attractiveness holds true in the research, which finds that narcissists are viewed as more attractive than the average person, and physical attractiveness is positively correlated with mirror gazing. A statistical analysis (called a meta-analysis) review of almost fifteen different studies comprised of over a thousand research participants revealed a small but reliable positive correlation between narcissism and physical attractiveness, according to observers' ratings of attractiveness (not the narcissists' rating themselves).[55] It's easy to imagine why narcissists rate themselves as more attractive, but why would they appear more attractive to others too? Narcissists do enjoy looking at themselves in the mirror. They may spend more time grooming themselves to bolster their grandiose self-images. In this way, narcissists may be more prone to self-objectify and identify with and to base their self-worth on their external appearance instead of their character.

And, physical attractiveness is positively correlated with mirror gazing. In one study, women who reported being satisfied with their appearance before mirror gazing felt even more attractive and confident after they gazed at themselves.[56] In an interesting field study, women and men were observed as they walked past a section of reflecting glass that served as a mirror.[57] Observers recorded the amount of time spent by each person gazing at his or her image as they walked by. The physical attractiveness of each participant was also rated separately by experimental observers. For both females and males, there was a positive correlation between the amount of time spent mirror-gazing and their physical attractiveness.

Research suggests that, like body dysmorphic disorder sufferers (discussed in part 2), narcissists often have a special relationship with the mirror. They use the mirror to narrow their focus solely to their physical image as a defense against feeling vulnerable and experiencing negative emotions. Narcissists use the mirror to validate their idealized self, but what would happen if they used the mirror to see beneath their surface appearance and get vulnerable instead?

PART VIII

Reflections on Loneliness, Aloneness, and Attachment

47. How Do You See Loneliness?

Have you ever felt lonely? I imagine the answer is yes. It seems that everyone has felt lonely at one time or another. Yet, each of us often feels that the experience is unique, which ironically isolates us all further! In this section, we will explore some of the common causes of loneliness and how our perception plays a critical role. You'll gather some insights into your unique relationship patterns and learn how to strengthen your relationship with yourself.

One way to think about loneliness is as a matter of perception. It is a state of distress or discomfort that you create when you *perceive* a gap between your desires for social connection and your actual experiences.

Some feelings of loneliness can be lessened simply by engaging in social activities. Maybe it's just a matter of finding someone to talk to or joining a social group. But the loneliness that people experience, chronically and over a long period, is often a result of a complex set of factors. Loneliness causes us to feel empty, isolated, and unwanted. We crave human contact, but our state of mind can actually make it more difficult to form connections with other people. This is because loneliness is not necessarily about being alone. Instead, we *feel* alone and isolated. In this way, loneliness is a state of mind. Simply put, we can create loneliness through our thinking, and lonely thinking perpetuates loneliness.

A study compared four of the most common treatments for loneliness: improving social skills, enhancing social support, increasing social interaction opportunities, and addressing faulty patterns of thought caused by chronic loneliness.[58] The results showed that changing thought patterns was the most effective.

So, if you're feeling lonely, consider how your automatic negative thoughts about others and social interactions might be getting in the way of making meaningful connections. Consider that these thoughts might not be accurate. Clear and compassionate self-awareness can help you break the cycle. That's the key ingredient to reducing loneliness.

Notice your thoughts and check in to see if your negative inner dialogue about your life and others' lives is accurate. Are you isolating yourself more? Do you feel unworthy of friendship? As discussed in previous chapters, when you observe negative thoughts that come up, practice the principle of mindfulness: keep your attention in the present, be open and curious, and adopt a kind intention toward yourself and those you are thinking about. Consider that these thoughts helped you stay safe earlier in your life but now are keeping you from having new, positive experiences. Stay present with yourself, be open to new possibilities, and approach them with kindness.

48. Loneliness on Your Face

Have you ever felt the urge to approach someone, but then you saw the look on their face and decided that it probably wasn't be a good idea? Our non-verbal cues and communication styles have a powerful effect on how others feel about approaching us.

In addition to negative and inaccurate thinking, research finds that lonely people give off nonverbal cues and engage in communication styles and social behavior that seem to maintain their state of loneliness. Some researchers hypothesize that loneliness is maintained by the inability to understand social signals, such as smiles and eye contact, that are key to positive social interactions. As a result, in our loneliness, we might fail to automatically mimic other people's facial expressions. For example, when we cross paths with someone, we may reflexively smile at each other briefly. Social mimicry naturally happens during most interactions, in which we automatically, and often unconsciously, mimic the emotional expressions of the person we are interacting with in face-to-face conversation. This is an important part of feeling connected, so without it we feel isolated—no matter how many people we engage with.

So, are lonely people intentionally not mimicking smiles and making eye contact, or is something else going on? To find out if lonely people pick up on these social cues and automatically mimic them, researchers at the University of California, San Diego, conducted a small, preliminary study with thirty-five student volunteers.[59] The students first completed three self-report questionnaires that measured their loneliness, depression, and extraversion. Based on the loneliness results, they were categorized as either lonely or not lonely. Next, they had electrodes attached to two pairs of their facial muscles that are important for generating emotional expressions—regions of the zygomaticus major, known as the smiling muscles, in the cheeks, and the corrugator supercilii, known as the frowning muscles, in the brow. The participants were then shown video clips of men and women making facial expressions of anger, fear, joy, and sadness.

When participants rated the facial expressions, the lonely and non-lonely students were equally good at distinguishing between facial expressions. There were no group differences in the strength of negative emotion ratings (anger, fear, and sadness) or positive ratings (joy). So the lonely people could recognize and understand emotional expressions just as well as the nonlonely group.

However, the lonely students' own faces spontaneously responded differently to the video clips. When members of both groups saw videos of people displaying anger, their own brows moved to mimic this expression automatically. But when the expression in the video was of joy, only the nonlonely group automatically smiled in response. The participants' scores on depression and extraversion were unrelated to this effect; only loneliness made the difference. The researchers verified that the lonely group could, in fact, deliberately mimic smiles and frowns when explicitly asked. They also found that the lonely group smiled automatically while viewing nonsocial positive images that did not include people (such as nature scenes) that also made the other group smile.

These findings suggest that failure to mimic other people's smiles automatically could play a role in maintaining loneliness. An inability to mimic a smile might send an antisocial signal to others, the researchers note, undermining social connections and leading to social disconnection. It could be an unconscious behavioral mechanism that maintains chronic loneliness.

It's important to note that this is a small, preliminary study. We can't infer a causal direction: Does loneliness interfere with smile mimicry, or does lack of smile mimicry create loneliness? But it does suggest that subtle nonverbal signals have a strong effect on whether others approach or avoid us. Increasing your awareness of these signals may improve the quality of your relationships.

- - - **try this** - - -

Think of people who make you smile. Practice thinking about them and practice smiling. Look in the mirror as you do this. Consider making a video journal describing a person you know who makes you smile or recall a social situation that makes you smile. Talk about it in your video journal and watch it back when you're feeling a bit lonely.

49. The Capacity to Be Alone

We've discussed loneliness, but what about just being alone with yourself? Do you feel content spending time by yourself?

Being comfortable alone is an essential skill that will increase your life quality by giving you more choices. When you're comfortable alone, you have more freedom to choose how you want to spend your time and with whom. It's more than just developing hobbies and interests and things to do when alone. Developing the capacity to be alone means developing a greater intimacy with yourself. Creating a stronger and more compassionate relationship with yourself is one of the main benefits of this self-reflection journey.

If you consider how our society is structured, it can be easy to imagine that you are all alone. But, if you've survived this far, you haven't done it all on your own. In fact, being with others is essential for our survival, and it's also key to developing the capacity to be alone.

In a classic essay, "The Capacity to Be Alone," psychoanalyst D. W. Winnicott described the paradox of aloneness in which he believed that the capacity to be alone develops from the experience of being alone in the presence of someone else (usually one's mother).[60] We need to feel the presence of another—someone who is there, with whom we feel safe, and who makes no demands on us. We need to be seen by others in this way to form a sense of ourselves. We need to know that another sees us and that we are separate from them simultaneously. This process assures us that we go on existing without their presence and that our existence has meaning and value. From this experience, we internalize a sense of self and safety that is a cornerstone of the ability to tolerate being alone with ourselves.

Experiencing someone being there for you unconditionally, who sees you with no expectations, no needs or demands, is essential. Having had such an experience early in life, you carry it with you throughout life. Without sufficient experience of being alone in the presence of another, we may come to associate aloneness with emptiness, fear, vulnerability, and lack of worthiness of others' attention or companionship. Suppose you miss out on having that experience in the early years. In that case, you can still get it from a therapist, mentor, or teacher—anyone who is willing to be unconditionally there for you and has your best interest at heart.

From this original experience, being alone in another's presence, we can create mental states that replicate the experience in our mind when we are alone. You can also have reminders of others that simulate what is called *the quiet presence of another.*

When I was a tween, I had a poster of Paul McCarthy in my bedroom. His eyes followed me everywhere, and that made me feel less lonely. It was a time when I couldn't quite relate to my parents, and finding a way to fit in with my peers was elusive and painful. But I had Paul's constant attention. He gazed at me pleasantly with his large soulful brown eyes. I didn't believe he was really there. I just needed him to see me. I imagined he understood me and was content just to be there and keep me company. It gave me solace. Now, like many people who spend hours a day working alone, I have photos of my loved ones on my desk—they keep me company—gazing at me pleasantly and mercifully demanding nothing as I work.

What function does this serve? The silent presence of loved ones provides a sense of constant comfort and connection. Without requiring the energy of an actual visit or a conversation, that energy can be directed toward the solitary work at hand. These photos looking back at us are a constant reminder that people care about us and are interested in us. Ultimately, they remind us of our humanity.

This quiet presence of another takes many forms. For instance, an artist may have a muse whose purpose is to inspire great work. In the artist's imagination, the muse doesn't demand anything but is often merely present, silent, and patiently *watching* as the artist works. Throughout history, these muses protected and *watched over* the artists and their creations. The quiet presence of another is also found in many spiritual traditions. People derive comfort from believing that God, spirits, angels, and deceased loved ones watch over them. When we are alone, we often think of those we love and imagine that they are with us. It is a private experience that many never talk about, but it's surprisingly common.

So, paradoxically, the capacity to be alone involves knowing that you never really are.

Do you have a person or a being who keeps you company when you are alone? Do you imagine them watching you, and if so, what is their general attitude toward you?

50. Attachment Patterns in Self-Relating

Your early experiences with your parents and caregivers influence your relationships later in life. It's a statement that is often heard in psychology. It makes intuitive sense, but often we don't realize the full extent of this influence. Attachment theory, initially proposed by John Bowlby, has helped many people better understand their relationships and how their past influences affect how they perceive themselves and others. The ideas of attachment theory are widely cited because they have proven useful in gaining insights into how we relate to others, particularly in romantic relationships. Here, I suggest that these same ideas can be applied to how you relate to *yourself.*

Let's review the theory first. Bowlby observed that all mammals, including humans, seem to have an innate drive to seek proximity and tender contact with their caregiver. This is particularly true when we feel threatened or afraid. Based on early experiences in seeking attachment, we develop expectations of how we believe others will respond to us in adulthood.

Those with a *secure attachment style* are comfortable relying on others and having others depend on them. They have a basic sense of trust and confidence that others will respond to them in a kind matter and that being close to others is safe and rewarding. You're likely to have a secure attachment style if you recall the majority of your childhood experiences as those that your parents met your security needs, and they comforted you and allowed you to be close to them, especially when you felt distressed, uncertain, or afraid.

There are two kinds of insecure attachment. If you have an *avoidant attachment style,* you generally avoid being close to others because you just don't see the benefits. You may worry that others might hurt you or let you down. So you don't make an effort to connect with them. You may come across as a bit aloof. An avoidant adult likely had childhood experiences in which they needed help or comfort and do not receive it. They may have had a parent who was physically or emotionally absent, been in a family where they were shamed for needing comfort, or been taken advantage of for showing vulnerability, to name a few. Over time the natural instinct to reach out for help and comfort from others shuts down because the act of reaching out gets either no response or negative results. It becomes too painful to keep relying on others who simply aren't there or cannot respond in a comforting way. So you tend to distance yourself from others generally and especially when you are stressed. If you're avoidant, you may worry about getting too close to others and not want them to see you vulnerable, and you may instinctively pull away from those close to you when you feel upset.

Those of you with an *anxious attachment style* are quite the opposite. You have a strong drive for closeness and worry that others will abandon you. You can be a bit clingy, which can, ironically, bring about your worst fear: repelling others away. Anxious types tend to be preoccupied with their relationships, feeling a mixture of excitement and dread. Excitement intensifies when things are going well. Dread looms when you start to worry that you may be suddenly abandoned, dropped, or rejected without warning. Anxious adults tend to have had childhoods imbued with a lot of unpredictability. Maybe one of your parents ran hot and cold, loving you intensely one minute and snapping at you and ridiculing you the next. Not knowing what might happen next, you learned to monitor your loved one's actions closely. You may have got caught in a pull-push or love-me versus love-me-not drama that may replicate (often unconsciously) in your adult relationships. For anxious types, love life and friendships are intense emotional roller coaster rides. They live in perpetual crises and drama. If you worry that others might abandon you and you tend to be preoccupied with your love life with lots of highs and lows, you might be the anxious attachment type.

Now let's take a step back. Before we start thinking about these attachment patterns in our relationships with others, let's consider how these patterns might play out in our relationship with ourselves. Your relationship with yourself is the longest and only truly ever-present relationship you have in life. It's the foundation of all your other relationships. You have witnessed every thought, dream, feeling, idea, and action you have ever had. No one has had your unique experience of life. Friendships and relationships can help you feel supported and loved, but a compassionate, loving connection to yourself, enjoying your time with yourself, and appreciating who you are even when others aren't around is the foundation for healthy, satisfying adult relationships.

A common adage is that if you like the person you're with (that is, yourself), you'll never feel lonely. What if loneliness is really a form of devaluing one's own company and abandoning yourself? In the next two chapters, we will explore the two forms of insecure attachment from the perspective of self-relating. That is, do you have an avoidant relationship with yourself? An anxious relationship with yourself? Or a secure one? Or maybe a combination?

- - - try this - - -

Think about the three different attachment styles. Which do you think best describes you and why? Take some time to reflect on this in your video journal. Recall past experiences and relationships that stand out in your mind.

---

51. Looking at Anxious Self-Attachment

In the anxious attachment pattern, you prefer to focus on and idealize others instead of looking at yourself and your own behavior. Early attachment experiences involved not being able to predict what the people you depended on might do, so you're anxious about getting your needs met and focus outward on what others are doing instead of checking in with yourself.

Kara came to see me for mirror meditation instruction. She had difficulty with traditional closed-eye meditation. Her mind drifted everywhere. At a silent meditation retreat, she went into a panic when she realized how difficult it was for her to suppress the impulse to talk to the people around her. She was quite uncomfortable spending time alone, and even in our session, she found it difficult to tolerate the lulls in conversation. She needed a lot of reassurance that it was okay for her to be there and that I valued her and our work together.

Kara is an example of the anxious self-relating pattern. She was preoccupied with herself but somehow not really there for herself either. Her attention flew and landed on different people in her life: monitoring her relationships with them, wondering what they would think of her being here with me, how they would do mirror meditation, what she was going to tell them about her experience of doing it, how she was going to have to deal with their criticisms and teasing and questioning about it, and on and on.

All this, of course, was happening in Kara's mind; her friends, family members, and current love interest weren't really there! Kara needed to face herself in a big way. Our work together involved helping her track her attention and notice the pattern of focusing on others instead of herself. Anxious attachment involves fear of abandonment. An anxious self-relating pattern is about *self-abandonment*. Instead of caring for yourself when you are feeling upset, you automatically focus on others and how they feel about you.

As Kara sat in front of the mirror, she naturally took other people's perspective in her life. She even asked me how I was experiencing it and apologized because it must be so boring for me to be with her while she was meditating. I assured her I was fine and happy to support her and encouraged her to keep bringing her focus back to herself.

Kara needed to develop more self-awareness around her habit of focusing on others. And at the same time, she needed to practice self-compassion. Sometimes, when we realize we are doing something self-defeating, we beat ourselves up further, making it even harder to change the habit. Our work together involved helping Kara stay with herself and notice her pattern of shifting her attention off of herself onto others and when and why she did it. I helped her track her attention to become more aware of the thoughts and feelings that immediately preceded her shift in awareness off herself onto monitoring someone else.

Kara realized she didn't feel safe with herself; she didn't trust herself or value her own company very much. I encouraged her to do a regular mirror meditation practice, just focusing on being with herself. "Just be with you. Only you. Only you. Just be with you." Over time her capacity to stay with herself, and not abandon herself to focus on others, grew.

A key to being comfortable with others is knowing that you don't have to do anything to keep another person there with you. If you're anxiously attached, you may believe other people will leave you if you don't constantly monitor their presence, moods, and reactions to you. So when you're alone with yourself, you tend to still be in that relationship-monitoring mode. It's essential to consider your loved ones' feelings and attitudes, but you also have to develop the capacity to take your focus off of them. You can practice this with yourself, by compassionately coming back to yourself time and time again.

- - - try this - - -

Next time you find your mind drifting to another person, when you are in meditation or otherwise, ask yourself: *What was I thinking or feeling right before that person popped into my mind? What do I want from this person? Love? Approval? Protection? Control over them?* Be as compassionately honest with yourself as you can. Remember that whatever your motives, wants, and needs are, they are human, and it is okay to have them, though it might not be wise to act on them! By being honest with yourself, you'll build self-trust and self-acceptance.

Also, see if there is a pattern in your needs and feelings: How can you support yourself to feel security, control, love, or approval when others aren't available?

Make a video journal to reflect on this. And, consider making a video journal when you are feeling secure and confident so you can watch it to reassure yourself when you're feeling more anxious and less secure.

52. Looking at Avoidant Self-Attachment

In the avoidant attachment pattern, you generally avoid being close to others. Another word for avoidant attachment is *dismissive*—you don't see relationships as that important. Because of early attachment experiences, you might come to believe that it's better to avoid other people, especially when you're stressed because they are likely to make things worse somehow. In terms of self-relating, avoidant people tend to be dismissive of themselves, by ignoring their feelings of distress—distracting themselves from themselves with work, videos, food, shopping, or whatever their favorite habit of keeping their attention off of themselves is. This automatic reflex developed to avoid the pain of feeling vulnerable and alone.

Tamara came for mirror meditation instruction because she felt something was missing in her life. She spent a lot of time alone and was generally comfortable with that. Yet, she felt that something was missing when she sat with herself in front of the mirror. Her attention drifted to her to-do list, organizing her closet, what she wanted to eat that day, the urge to shop for something online—anything but herself! Though this was not a huge problem for her in day-to-day life, she noticed that she automatically avoided looking at herself and could not reach out to others when she felt stressed. As a child, she was teased or ignored for being vulnerable. As an adult, she thought it was only acceptable to reach out to others when she felt totally together. She admitted her relationships weren't very deep or satisfying for her.

Our work involved helping Tamara stay with herself, not dismissing or avoiding herself, no matter how she was feeling. At first, Tamara felt nothing. Her attention was like a cork in water: it kept coming up to the surface instead of dropping deeper into her feelings. She had learned to keep everything on the surface. "I don't feel anything," she would say. I said, "It's okay. Stay with yourself and simply watch yourself."

It was hard for her to let me see her. She worried I might force her to feel something or interpret her feelings in inaccurate, wrong, or simply annoying ways. I assured her that she was the authority on how she felt and that I had no expectation around it. I was merely holding space for her to have a new experience with herself—whatever that might be. I encouraged her to do mirror meditation alone and pointed out that it was also vital for her to let others she trusted see her vulnerability a bit. In the avoidant pattern, people disregard their feelings when under stress and disconnect further from others who might provide valuable reflection and support. Letting go of this habit would help Tamara develop deeper friendships.

As she was able to stay with herself and watch herself, she eventually started to feel. She began to worry that she might start to feel too much and become too overwhelmed or so involved in her feelings so that she wouldn't be able to get things done. I suggested that she do mirror meditation for ten minutes a day and practice staying with herself and letting herself feel. After the ten minutes, she should do whatever else she wanted or had to do, but to just commit to be with herself every day for the ten minutes no matter what. She also agreed to make a ten-minute video journal every day and talk about her feelings even if she felt nothing.

By committing to give herself this attention daily, she built a stronger relationship with herself over time. She discovered some deep emotions that she'd been avoiding. Eventually, self-compassion began to upwell in her when she realized just how much she actually felt and how she'd been avoiding herself and her true feelings for so long.

- - - try this - - -

Next time you are in a state of not feeling much, watch yourself in the mirror. See if you can tolerate being with yourself without feeling much.

Notice when you feel the urge to snack, scroll, shop, or whatever your favorite distraction is, and see if you can check yourself out in the mirror instead, even if it's just a passing glance to interrupt the habit.

See if you can get in the habit of checking in with yourself when you're feeling stressed instead of abandoning yourself. Know that you can simply sit with yourself; you don't have to fix yourself and change your feelings; just be there for yourself.

PART IX

Risk Being Seen

53. Others Are Our Mirrors

As social beings, we look at others to reflect who we are. This starts from day one with our parents and expands as we grow. How could we possibly understand who we are if it wasn't for others reflecting us and telling us who we are, their reactions to our physical form and emotions, and how they reflect, mirror, and mimic us? Through these experiences, we form a sense of self.

Having people around who are loving, conscientious, and accurate observers and reflectors is terrific. But, it's also entirely possible to be raised by adults who cannot offer loving, reality-based, and consistent reflections. Most of us have had both kinds of experiences. Can you recall a time when you were young and an adult told you something about yourself that stayed with you and changed your view of yourself? Was it accurate? Was it kind?

When you were just forming your sense of self and your identity as a child, you could not question the accuracy of these reflections. You simply took them in as facts. In general, children are much more vulnerable to negative messages than adults are. For instance, if you tell a child, "Hey, you're stupid!" the child is much more likely to believe it's true and take it to heart. In contrast, if you say to an adult, "Hey! You're stupid!" you can expect some pushback! As adults, we have the emotional and cognitive capacity to go back over and reexamine our beliefs about ourselves. We can note where they came from and question their accuracy. It's easier for adults to reject inaccurate reflections and erroneous feedback. Our sense of self is more solid in adulthood, but it's built on the foundation of the messages we received about ourselves as children.

In part 3, we began to work with self-talk with special attention to the inner critic. In this section, we'll focus on the dynamics of how being seen by others influences your perception of yourself. I also share some stories that illustrate common issues many of us encounter when we risk being seen. We'll discuss why it's essential not to let fear of being seen keep you from fully engaging in life. There is no guarantee that we'll be seen and reflected with accuracy or kindness, but you can find encouragement to keep connecting with others as you stay connected to yourself. In the chapters to come, you'll find tips and techniques to improve your ability to let yourself be seen—and make it easier for others to connect with you in fulfilling ways.

- - - try this - - -

In your video journal, discuss how others' reflections of you have influenced you. Think back on your life. What were you told about yourself when you were growing up? What words did adults or other children use to describe you? What did they say about you? How has it affected you as an adult? Then consider:

How have you been seen in the past? Positively or negatively? Accurately or not?

How has it affected you?

How do you want to be seen now in the present? In the future?

54. Reflections That Shape Your Identity

Mirror meditators often remark how they see some resemblance of one of their relatives when they look at themselves in the mirror thoughtfully over time. "I see my mother looking back at me." "This is definitely my father's nose." "I see my grandma's twinkle in my eyes!" These revelations often lead them to contemplate how their appearance has shaped their view of themselves and their identity.

I've devoted a good deal of time to contemplating my identity in the mirror. I grew up always knowing that I was adopted. My father told me that he wanted a little girl with blonde hair and blue eyes, and when he saw me, he knew I was the one. So as a child, I imagined my parents going to the baby store, wandering through the aisles searching, then seeing me there on the shelf (usually the top self), and exclaiming with glee, "There she is! She's the one!" They then took me down from the shelf, put me in the shopping cart, went through the checkout line, and took me home. Being called "Barbie" further drove home the message that my appearance mattered—a lot!

My appearance, like everyone's, is largely an accident of birth. Our features can be altered to some degree, but those salient characteristics that people often judge us on—like skin color, height, age, and facial features related to race and ethnicity—are hard to change. So we are stuck with our appearance to some degree, and it often plays a crucial role in our fate. So how do we come to terms with this?

Contemplating my image in the mirror over the years, I was always sure I wasn't "Barbara" and certainly not "Barbie!" But who was I, really? To answer that question, I decided to find my birth parents. It was quite the adventure. Meeting them was fascinating and life-changing. Just knowing the story of their lives and my ancestors gave me a sense of completeness and integration I hadn't felt before. But I found *seeing* them face-to-face to be deeply satisfying. They gave me photos of themselves at different ages and of their parents and siblings. I saw the remarkable resemblances. For the first time in my life, I saw people who indeed looked like me. I compared my image in the mirror to the photos with the delight and fascination of the child. It might have seemed silly or vain to an observer, but for me, it was a profound shift in how I saw myself.

Meeting my birth parents affirmed so much of what I inherently knew about myself that was never reflected back to me by my adopted parents or other adults when I was growing up. It increased my appreciation for life and affirmed my sense of purpose. After that revelation, sitting in front of the mirror thinking of myself as "Barbara" began to feel excruciating—the name echoed false deep in my bones. I could not avoid seeing it, and therefore, I could not avoid feeling it. Eventually, I changed my name to "Tara," which resonates deeply true in me.

We all have at least one story about how someone's perception of you profoundly molded your identity. What's your story?

When you look in the mirror for an extended period, you may start to see these different aspects of yourself. You may have different identities based on language; ethnicity and religion; social, political, and ideological beliefs; gender; sexual orientation; as well as sports and a wide array of other interests. Your different identities can be kept separate through the anonymity of society, social media, and the transient nature of social interactions. Yet, at the same time, you may have a deep desire to be seen, known, and accepted for who you are in your entirety.

The mirror can help you increase your awareness of any identity discrepancies. For instance, people often remark that they feel much younger than they look. Seeing your own face may be a poignant reminder of wanting to look different and the stories that go with that desire. I encourage you to take the time to look and to listen to what your image is telling you. Then, you can use the mirror to come to terms with those uncomfortable aspects of yourself and integrate them into a solid sense of self.

- - - **try this** - - -

Consider the stories you were told growing up about your appearance. Next, recall life experiences in which your physical appearance played a role in your fate. Then, make some video journals about these experiences and describe how they've impacted you.

55. Self-Objectification Revisited

In many ways, I was lucky. My physical characteristics were considered desirable. But, I've often wondered: *What if I were born with darker hair or darker skin? What if one of my fingers or toes were missing? What if I had some disability and did not function as a normal healthy infant? Would I have been left on the shelf? Maybe I would not have been taken home by anyone.*

Whether we like it or not, in life, we play roles: we make contracts with people to be things for them, be it a happy daughter, a loyal husband, a brilliant student, an ambitious employee, a caring mother, and the list goes on.

try this

Take a moment to jot down what comes to mind when you consider the roles you play in your life. Then for each role, consider:

Is your physical appearance is related to the role?

Do you enjoy playing this role?

What is the primary emotion you feel in the role? Love? Sadness? Anger?

Who are you playing the role for?

What are you getting for playing it?

How is this role reflected back to you?

Does the role fit you? Do you want to play this role?

Try this exercise to contemplate the roles you play in the mirror or make a video journal discussing your roles. Then watch it back mindfully and see what insight you gain.

You may have a specific persona you put on. For instance, if you have a spouse and young children, you probably don't act the same when you are with your spouse as you do with your children. Likewise, you don't talk to your employer the same way you talk to your best friend or mother. Can you see that difference in the mirror? That is, are you becoming a slightly different person?

Begin your mirror meditation with some body centering and slow deep breathing, and then bring specific personas to mind as you look at yourself. Next, say your name in relation to that role aloud, be it "Mommy," "Sweetheart," "Dr. Cunningham," "Bobby," "Robert," "Ma'am," or whatever unique nicknames you might have. Say your name and experience what it feels like as you look at yourself, being open, curious, and kind to yourself.

You may have inadvertently participated in a naturalistic study of seeing your different roles. When the pandemic forced the world to switch to video conferencing instead of in-person interactions, many people discovered their discomfort with seeing themselves in different roles at work or talking to a friend on camera. They got distracted. It seemed that looking at themselves created a sense of discord and was even a bit jarring.

Early on, because of my research on reflections, several journalists tapped me for insights on how the loss of face-to-face interactions and increase in video conferencing might affect us psychologically. For years, I'd been using the mirror to help people overcome appearance-related self-criticism and get more comfortable with themselves in general. So when reporters began soliciting advice on how people should deal with seeing themselves on Zoom, I suggested they embrace it. We should all take time to look at ourselves with compassion before the call begins, I said. See others and let them see you; we're all in this together.

Apparently, this wasn't what they wanted to hear. My suggestions were drowned out by quick fixes to buffer the intimate intensity of the Zoom space, tips like "move further from the camera" and instructions for how to hide your own image. Zoom fatigue received a lot of attention, with the focus on how exhausting it is to see too many faces, too close with full-frontal emotions and nonverbal cues out of context.

But I embraced seeing my own image on Zoom. Though looking at myself in the camera was not exactly a walk in the park; in contrast to the radiant, youthful faces of my nineteen-year-old students, my middle-aged face looked tired and worn. But there was something important to be gained by not shying away from my own reflection. Given the backdrop of those dire times and the immediate challenge to connect with my students, I refused to be distracted by my own imperfections. It was time to practice what I'd been preaching about self-acceptance and self-compassion—and allow myself to be seen exactly as I was.

This approach had some surprising benefits. In contrast to the classroom, the direct facial feedback on Zoom allowed me to learn so much about how what I was saying impacted my students' moment to moment. For example, I could not help but notice a slight frown when I unintentionally cut a student off in my eagerness to make a point or the smiles of recognition when I first joined the meeting.

I came to enjoy the increased real-time feedback, and soon I was also watching every lecture recording. At times, I realized I had misspoken or forgotten to relay something important. Without reviewing the recording, I wouldn't have known to correct these mistakes during subsequent sessions.

The sudden switch to Zoom also involved inviting students into my home quite literally. This switch was also an awakening for people to realize the different roles they play—the separateness or the overlap. Do you feel like a professor wearing your PJ bottoms? How do your feelings about yourself change when your cat photobombs an important business call? So many of us saw ourselves in these roles very differently from home and on-camera—what an excellent opportunity for integration.

56. Gaslighting

How others reflect us can be distorted by their own agendas. One of the common distortions is known as gaslighting. The term gaslighting comes from 1930s play and movie adaptations by the same name. In the plot, the husband attempts to convince his wife that she is going insane by manipulating small things in their environment and insisting that she is mistaken, misremembering things, or delusional when she points out these changes. At one point, the husband slowly dims the gas lights in their home while pretending nothing has changed to make his wife doubt her own perceptions.

The term gaslighting is now commonly used to describe efforts to manipulate someone's perception of reality. First, however, it's important to note there is a range of gaslighting behavior from the cold, calculating examples in the original play to milder forms. In some cases, people might not even be aware that they are doing it.

Gaslighting works based on the psychological principle of cognitive dissonance. Cognitive dissonance is the idea that you cannot hold to two conflicting beliefs simultaneously without creating discomfort (or dissonance).

Let's take a typical example of everyday gaslighting. A mother yells at her child. The mother believes that she is a good, caring mother, and she just yelled at her child, who is now crying. These are incompatible facts: How can she be a good mother and yell at the same time? She needs to shift something: Maybe she's not a good mother after all? Or, maybe she really didn't yell; she just raised her voice a little bit, and her son was just too sensitive and overacted. Then he asks, "Mommy, why did you yell at me?" through his tears. He is also experiencing cognitive dissonance: he believes his mother is safe and will not hurt him. But she just did hurt him by yelling. Then his mother replies, "I didn't yell at you! You're just too sensitive!" His dissonance is resolved: his mother is good and safe, he is too sensitive, and there is no reason for him to be crying.

They are both totally gas-lit. The mother believes she is a good mother, so she's not motivated to change her angry behavior. For her son to maintain his belief that his mother is good and safe, he must disregard his own feelings and genuine reactions to her behavior. He may generalize that and learn to distrust his gut feelings and natural responses, believing he is just too sensitive or overreacting when others verbally abuse him. He may think that even if people yell at him, they somehow are still safe and have his best interest at heart.

As children, we can be especially vulnerable to developing distortions based on what our parents tell us is accurate. Throughout life, we look to others to confirm our reality. It's easy to see how we can lose track of our true feelings and genuine reactions over time. We want to believe that we are safe and loved—we don't want to be uncomfortable—but often, the state of discomfort is what we must experience to see the truth and grow.

Cognitive dissonance can prevent us from seeing the truth by keeping erroneous beliefs in place. For example, you might have noticed that there are times when you don't want to look at yourself in the mirror. Consider if this is because looking at yourself would generate some cognitive dissonance.

For instance, Brad believed he was in a happy, committed relationship. But, the mirror in his hallway told a different story. When his partner was around, Brad would catch a glimpse of himself in the mirror and notice his face pinched in annoyance, but his face appeared smooth and serene when his partner was away. Brad even caught himself making a tight phony smile when he greeted his partner in the hall. But, Brad wasn't ready to examine his beliefs about his relationship, so he started to think the mirror was outdated and replaced it with new artwork that had a nonreflective surface.

It's okay if you don't want to confront every aspect of yourself and your beliefs at once. But developing awareness—and accepting that you're not ready to look at something—can often be the most compassionate response you can have toward caring for yourself. You can care for yourself and be committed to growing simultaneously: these are two beliefs that need not be incompatible!

57. Be Consistent to Build Trust

If your feelings weren't seen and accurately reflected, you may have developed certain ways of coping that don't really serve you. For example, in part 6, we met Amber. She dealt with difficulties recognizing, understanding, and expressing her feelings because her parents did not validate her so-called "negative" feelings when she was growing up. Another way an early lack of reflection can manifest is when you exaggerate crises, traumas, and difficulties. To observers, your reaction can look way out of proportion to what's happening. But it is often a learned way of communicating danger or distress that has worked in the past.

For instance, Amy was frequently labeled a "drama queen," "princess," or even a "bitch." Whenever there was a problem—be it with family and friends, her romantic partner, or customer service representatives—Amy made a big deal out of it.

When she first noticed a problem, her anxiety spiked, which often led her to panic. It seemed when Amy saw a potential problem for which she knew she had to reach out for help, she became anxious and doubted that anyone would be there to help her. As a reaction to that belief, she started to exaggerate the problem to make it easier to convince others that it was serious. Unfortunately, this strategy often backfired as it made people annoyed and doubtful of her claims. *Amy was not letting her distress be seen in a way that got her the support she needed.*

As we worked together, she came to notice how helpless she felt when problems first arose. By making things more dramatic, she felt a sense of control even though the control was often an illusion. She traced this habit back to her childhood when her parents did not believe her when she complained and when they ignored or trivialized her distress. Now, as an adult, she figured that the only way to get others to see there was a problem was to make them as uncomfortable as she was. So, as a consequence, when Amy was distressed, everyone tended to avoid her, which was ironically her worst fear.

How could Amy break the cycle? Through mirror meditation and video journaling, she practiced witnessing herself in various states of distress. Amy made videos of herself in a rambling panic, enraged and confused, blaming others and saying mean things about them, and so on. Later, when she was in a calm, centered space, Amy watched her videos mindfully. She felt an array of emotions as she watched herself, from annoyance to embarrassment to helplessness to compassion. She realized that these displays of intense distress were creating more stress for everyone.

Studying her video journals, Amy gained an understanding of her reactions. She became more aware of when she was about to spin out into an exaggerated reaction. Amy learned to pause, breathe, ground and center, and make a short video practicing some calming self-talk. With practice, she was able to calm herself down before she reached out for help.

But the challenge of asking for help was still looming. I suggested that Amy first practice a good dose of self-acceptance. She would probably never be a super chill person, but she could be accurate and consistent. Often Amy started to exaggerate and amp up her intensity when she felt people were judging her or doubting her claims. I suggested that Amy trust herself and practice rigorous honesty. The issue may be an error on her credit card statement, a comment her boyfriend made that didn't sit right with her, or a request from her mother that seemed inconsiderate. Amy noticed that she often doubted her reactions when others started to question them. She then went into overdrive.

Amy realized that she was looking for her feelings to be validated when she was upset and trying to solve the problem simultaneously. Often, that was too overwhelming for others. I suggested that she separate her reaction from the problem. Getting her response validated was entirely different from getting the problem solved. Often Amy would have her big reaction, others would become annoyed and withdraw from her, and she'd be all alone with her problem. Instead, I encouraged her to trust her ability to detect problems.

When she thought about it, it was rare that she ever imagined a problem. But often, it was the case that she saw the problem before others did. Amy had an early-warning system. One of her more insightful friends called her "a canary in the coal mine" to describe her ability to see the danger before others did. This sensitivity was a valuable skill that Amy had to learn to use wisely.

The key was being consistent. When there was a problem, Amy would have a strong reaction, and she had to keep pursuing a solution no matter what others' judgment was about her or the situation. Instead of backing down in frustration or exaggerating and intensifying things, she learned to stay with herself and the problem at hand consistently.

By knowing who you are and letting yourself be seen—consistently—you build self-trust, and others will trust you to be you. If you hide your genuine reactions or alter them to get a specific response from others, you'll undermine both your self-trust and the trust others have in you. Abraham Lincoln is quoted as saying, "Whoever you are, be a good one." I would add, "be a good one and a consistent one."

Amy knew she'd never be a super laid-back person. But she was able to build more trustworthy relationships by responding consistently. She learned to accept her strong reactions and separate her reaction from finding a solution. As a result, she found people who would support her consistently and appreciate her sensitivity.

58. If You Really Knew Me

After a painful breakup, Vanessa was determined to change her approach to dating. She spent hours watching YouTube videos on dating tips. She couldn't resist clicking on videos with titles like "Make Any Man Fall in Love with You" and "Avoid These Behaviors That Turn Men Off Instantly." Then, she took an online course called "The Man Magnet." It was a total game-changer. She learned how to act in a very confident and seductive manner. She practiced sensual body language and how to converse and flirt with men in a way that drove them wild. Finding Vanessa irresistible, men began to flock, and she thoroughly enjoyed all the attention.

Eventually, she drew Scott into her orbit. After few months into their hot love affair, they decided to move in together—and that's when everything changed. Scott fell in love with Vanessa's sexy, seductive man-magnet persona. He hadn't yet seen her other sides, like when she had a cold, or felt fat, or was cranky because she hadn't slept well. Scott hadn't really noticed how hard Vanessa worked behind the scenes to make her very successful career look easy. He hadn't seen her anxious moments or bouts of insecurity as she dealt with people and problems that came up in her everyday life. Actually, Scott didn't want to see those parts of her—he wanted to see a sexy girlfriend who effortlessly kept her successful business going and was always in a playful, generous mood.

So when Vanessa was upset or not feeling as attractive as usual, he tried not to notice, hoping the moment would pass and his fun, sexy girlfriend would come back. Vanessa knew that Scott wasn't paying much attention when she was in a bad mood. If she tried to tell him about something on her mind that was troubling her, he'd change the subject to something light, sexy, and fun. Scott wasn't a bad guy; he just didn't realize that Vanessa had many facets and that she simply couldn't be a man magnet 24/7.

Scott's behavior triggered feelings of anxiety and shame in Vanessa. She started to believe that she wasn't just a person in a bad mood but that she was a bad person for letting her partner down and being such a downer. She started to judge herself as "selfish" when she wanted to just chill in her yoga pants and eat ice cream instead of putting on her man-magnet routine for Scott.

Like many of us, Vanessa had an "if you really knew me" script in her mind that got activated when she became more intimate and revealed more of herself to someone special. Many people often believe that if others saw who they really are, they'd be rejected. So you may feel especially vulnerable showing the less flattering aspects of yourself, and your partner's reaction can have a considerable impact.

After Vanessa and Scott broke up, she realized how much she struggled with letting herself be seen for who she truly was. To her, the situation was hopeless: To maintain a romantic relationship, she had to act a certain way all the time, which was impossible. But, if she showed who she truly was, she'd be rejected.

I suggested that Vanessa use mirror meditation to get really comfortable with who she was—and realize that not every man was going to like her. She had wanted every man to fall in love with her to soothe her bruised ego after her last breakup. But, to find a more satisfying relationship, she needed to reframe her approach to dating.

To know whether a man was compatible with her, Vanessa had to show her authentic self early in the dating experience. I reasoned with her that discovering incompatibility on the first or second date is a lot easier to deal with than realizing you're not suitable for each other several months or a year or so down the road.

What did Vanessa want in a relationship? Passion, acceptance, affirmation, compliments, ultimately someone who could see her clearly but also kindly. She wanted a man who would accept her and love her for who she really was.

So as she did her mirror meditation practice, she simply sat with herself and gave herself the reflection she'd hoped to get from a man. She talked in video journals in the way she wanted to talk with her man at the end of the day, sharing her thoughts, feelings, and plans for the future. She practiced being herself, with herself.

As she watched her videos, she realized how much depth of feeling and the insights she had to share with another. So why was she spreading herself so thin? Why was she superficially trying to get every man in the world to fall in love with her?

When she began looking for another man, she enjoyed turning on her man magnet to attract possible partners, and then as Vanessa got to know them, she made sure to show other sides of herself too. She was still aware of how men reacted to her, but she made a point to really see them too. Instead of manipulating them with her sexiness to get them to respond to her in the way she wanted, she got curious about who they really were and how they genuinely felt. It became apparent if they weren't open to seeing her authentic self. If he only wanted to see a caricature of a sexy man magnet, she stopped dating him and moved on. She eventually found Pierre, a man she could totally be herself with. He appreciated her complexity—he saw the different facets of her and loved and accepted them all.

Seeing yourself and allowing yourself to be seen by others takes practice. When you allow yourself to be seen, you give others the freedom to reveal themselves too.

59. Trust Yourself to Be Seen

Other people's gazes and their accompanying judgments can be tremendously powerful. So it makes sense that you'd hesitate to be seen. But, if you want to influence others, to change the world, or to just change a few people's minds about something you care about, then you need to get comfortable being seen. Likewise, if you want to be loved and known for who you truly are, you have to get comfortable being seen as you truly are.

Knowing who you are and having a regular practice like mirror meditation and video journaling can help you feel more confident being seen. As you get more comfortable seeing yourself in the mirror, you'll notice aspects of yourself that you hadn't seen before. Most of us are more complex than we realize. When you thoroughly know yourself, you'll be much less likely to be blindsided by others' comments and reflections about you.

"Happiness is when what you think, what you say, and what you do are in harmony." This quote, attributed to Mahatma Gandhi, is, in my view, the perfect definition for authenticity and integrity combined. After all, the word "integrity" comes from the word integration. Therefore, having the courage to show up and be seen builds integrity.

The Johari window is a technique that helps people better understand their relationship with themselves and others. The Johari window has four quadrants for your self-view.

Those aspects of yourself that you know about, and others do too. (Open)

Those aspects of yourself that you know about, but others do not. (Hidden)

Those aspects of yourself that you don't know about, but others do. (*Blind*)

Those aspects of yourself that you and others do not know. (Unknown)

Others observe you from their own vantage point, so it's bound to be different from your own. Finding people who are willing to give you honest accurate feedback about how they see you is precious. Being open to receiving their impressions of you can help you illuminate blind spots.

- - - try this - - -

You can explore seeing yourself in different contexts and letting yourself be seen. Here are some suggestions.

1. Regularly videotape your Zoom calls. Review them with an eye toward your facial expressions and nonverbal behavior. Notice how others interact with you; slow down the video and mindfully look. What kind of insights and emotions came to you from seeing yourself on video interacting with others?

2. Agree to let people look at you with no agenda but to look for a specific time period. No talking and no touching. Just looking. Try designating a minute or two, working up to ten minutes to just allowing yourself to be looked at by another person. You can do this in a variety of contexts.

   In my seminars, where public speaking is a component, I have each student stand in front of the class and just allow themselves to be looked at. It can be extremely nerve-racking—and also incredibly liberating. You come to realize sticks and stones may break your bones, but a gaze can never hurt you.

3. Have a looking date with your romantic partner. A looking date is an excellent idea if you're sexually or physically intimate with someone and you find yourself wanting to avoid them seeing you and your body, for example, by having sex with the lights out. Instead, try letting your partner look at you with no words and no touching—experiment with wearing different amounts of clothing. Let their eyes rove around all over you. What was it like to allow yourself to be seen in this intimate way? Then, switch and look at them. Then share your experience with your partner.

4. Think of the role you play in life that makes you feel the proudest. Allow those that you serve to admire you. No, it's not narcissistic; it fulfills a human need we have to admire others. This acknowledgment can be simple, like pausing when someone compliments you, really noticing them seeing you. If you are a parent or a leader, notice how others look to you for guidance; pause and allow yourself to be looked up to.

5. If you encounter someone who thinks you look beautiful, pause and allow yourself to be seen as beautiful.

6. What if you notice others seeing something unfavorable or inaccurate? Being able to differentiate others' projections from your own view of yourself is essential. Seeing someone look at you with scorn or suspicion, or whatever your worst fear, may be challenging. If you can tolerate it, you'll find it can be incredibly liberating too! Instead of hiding, you can learn to tolerate people seeing you inaccurately. It's okay. You don't have to hide or become invisible or argue for your right to be seen accurately. You can see them seeing you and allow yourself to be seen however imperfect it may be. In the next section, we'll examine how your own projections can get in the way of seeing others accurately.

PART X

See Others with Clarity and Compassion

60. Seeing Others: What Are You Looking For?

Years ago, I attended a workshop where we did a warm-up exercise I'll never forget. The instructor asked us to mill around and then stop and turn to the nearest person and ask, "Are you?" The person was instructed to say nothing in return. Everyone experienced what it was like to ask, "Are you?" to a variety of people whom they hadn't met yet. We were all on the receiving end of the question many times too. The space between the question and no answer was illuminating. It brought to my awareness what I think others always seem to want from me. And, I realized what I always seem to be looking for in them. That pause profoundly changed how I viewed my exchanges with others. I felt the deep discomfort of others' (often imagined) expectations of me. And, I realized how easy it was for me to judge a person before they had even said a word.

Can you think of the last time someone did not respond to your email, text, or call within the timeframe that you thought they should? What kinds of thoughts went through your mind? You've probably had the experience of expecting the worst as you wait for the text bubbles on your phone to turn into words. Our worst fears about others can often seep into these pauses in communication. When information is lacking, our minds can start to think the worst.

You've done a considerable amount of hard work to increase your self-awareness and self-compassion. We will now consider how you can apply this knowledge to see the other people in your life. In this final section, we'll look at the psychology of seeing others with clarity and compassion. Our view of the world and its people is shaped by our past experiences, beliefs, current needs, and desires, to name but a few sources. We can probably never be totally objective, but we can be aware of our biases and expand our views. Some common biases get in the way of us seeing others accurately and kindly.

In any social situation, we simply can't process all the information that is available to us. So we have developed certain cognitive shortcuts to help us understand the social environment. Some of these shortcuts are tremendously helpful, while others can get us into trouble. Social psychologists have identified various perceptual biases we have when we are interacting and trying to understand others. One is the confirmation bias: the idea is that we have an assumption or a set of assumptions about someone. These preconceived ideas tend to guide your conversation topics and behavior so you can confirm your assumptions are correct. We look for information about people to verify our assumptions about them. Disconfirming information would create cognitive dissonance that would lead us to change our beliefs about the person. Though, in theory, that might seem like a good idea, we like having a sense of prediction and control. Feeling as though you know who someone is and what to expect from them (even if it's wrong or unpleasant) can often feel better than dealing with uncertainty.

We use labels to help us understand other people and their motivations. Often these labels aren't really accurate but are convenient ways to help us manage our anxiety and expectations about others. Here are some scenarios that might be relatable.

Labeling a man as "a player" might mean he has sexual energy and confidence. You might find it intriguing and disturbing at the same time. Labeling him a player gives you a sense of control to not fall for his charms. In truth, the man has confidence and was attracted to you but now feels judged.

Labeling someone "an a**hole" might come about when they have done something that has caused you pain or great inconvenience and they appear entirely oblivious to it. But, in reality, this person has made a mistake that caused you pain that they were unaware of; they are now trying to correct the error but finding it extremely difficult because you're calling them names.

Labeling a woman "a witch" might mean that you perceive her as not following the rules of good conduct you expect from women. Her behavior is powerful and unpredictable, and you find it threatening. In reality, the woman doesn't follow gender stereotypes and is not interested in doing things to make you more comfortable with who she is.

We make casual assumptions about people all the time. For example, imagine you walk into a room and trip. You are likely to look around to see what it was in the environment that made you trip. But, an observer would be more likely just to think you're clumsy. This way of interpreting behavior is called the fundamental attribution error. When we try to understand and explain our own behavior, especially if it's something unfavorable, we tend to look for external circumstances, like water on the floor or an untied shoelace. When we try to understand and explain the behavior of others, we tend to focus on their internal characteristics, like being clumsy, spacey, or careless. When we look at others, we see them more prominently than the context. But, with oursevles, we can see the context much more readily.

What we focus on is usually related to our very human needs that have been shaped by evolution. We want to ward off threats from the environment and form and maintain social bonds that are the most advantageous. Here we'll consider the possibility of mindfully shifting our focus from looking for threats to being visually curious. This section is full of insights and suggestions for seeing others with more compassion and clarity. We'll discuss the power of eye contact and how to see others compassionately and help them without getting overwhelmed. We will also look at common biases and negative emotions that we may use as defenses to keep from feeling anxious but that really end up creating great distance between ourselves and others. Understanding your own biases and the ways you may misperceive others may help improve your relationships tremendously.

61. Looking Through the Eyes of Love

The public debut of mirror meditation, as a group experience, took place at the Rubin Museum of Art in New York City in 2016. Sixty people curious to try this new form of meditation gathered in the sacred shrine of the museum. In silence, they took their seats at either side of a long table. A feeling of sacredness and reverence was in the air. After settling in, they lifted the black cover from their portrait mirror and began to gaze at themselves. Though the museum held many exquisite gems, they directed their gaze solely on the treasure right in front of them in the mirror.

I led them through a mirror meditation to release their judgments and relax into self-acceptance and then to consider seeing themselves with compassion. As the meditation went deeper, I received divine inspiration to ask them to lift their gaze and look at the person (usually a stranger) across from them. Suddenly, everything felt lighter. Eyes twinkled, and smiles erupted. Everything became sparkly and magical. You may have heard the saying, "Many hands make light the work." In this moment, it seemed that *many eyes made light the work*. As I witnessed the power of this group willing to see each other with kindness, I knew why they say the eyes are the window to the soul.

What is it about looking into someone's eyes that's so scary and intriguing at the same time?

Our eyes are our most expressive facial feature. They can communicate a range of social cues and emotions, which can profoundly influence your social interactions. Looking directly or averting our gaze has powerful consequences. Research finds that direct gaze is associated with confidence, interest, and attraction, while an averted gaze of looking away is related to lack of confidence, rejection, and being socially ostracized.[61] In addition, many people consider eye contact to be a sign of trustworthiness. We are more likely to believe a person who's looking straight at us. On the other hand, not looking someone in the eye is often associated with lying. So, if you want to build trust with another person, you have to be comfortable making eye contact.

We look at people's eyes for essential information about their emotional state. Twenty years ago, a team of scientists at the University of Cambridge developed a test called "Reading the Mind in the Eyes" (or the Eyes Test, for short). The test consists of a series of photo snippets of people's eyes only.[62] The test revealed that people could rapidly interpret what another person thinks or feels from looking at their eyes alone. They did not need information from the mouth area or other parts of the face to accurately read their emotional state. It also showed that some of us are better at this than others. On average, women score better on this test than men. Accuracy on the test is related to self-reported cognitive empathy, accurate perception of emotion in full facial expressions, and breadth of vocabulary. I think that finding is absolutely stupendous! It's no wonder eye contact is so impactful. It can trigger a personal connection, even if it lasts for only a few seconds.

Eye gazing takes eye contact one step further. Eye gazing is the act of looking into someone's eyes for an extended amount of time. It's a powerful, intimate practice that can help you become closer to another person. It's beneficial for fostering even deeper connections. Prolonged eye contact can also benefit your social relationships because it gives you practice recognizing and understanding another's emotions.

We bond emotionally as we gaze into each other's eyes. The hormone oxytocin helps this process along. Oxytocin has been called "the cuddle hormone" or "the love hormone" due to its association with pair-bonding and feelings of warmth, desire to be close, and trust. Oxytocin helps reinforce the early attachment between mothers and their infants and the bonds between romantic partners.

Recent research shows oxytocin plays a role in how we bond with our dogs too.[63] Mutual gazing increases oxytocin levels in both humans and dogs. When dogs sniffed oxytocin, they increased eye gazing, and that had a positive effect on their owners. So, if another human is not available to eye gaze, consider looking into the soulful eyes of your dog!

As a dedicated practice, eye gazing has a rich history. People have been doing it for centuries to deepen their sexual and spiritual connection. Tantra is an ancient philosophy based on Hinduism and Buddhism. The practice is about achieving spiritual enlightenment through meditation, mantras, and rituals. Tantric eye gazing is one technique passed down through the ages. During Tantric eye gazing, you look deeply into your partner's eyes to foster a spiritual and sexual connection.

There are many ways to do eye gazing. Here's one basic method.

1. *Sit in a comfortable position and face your partner.*

2. *Set a timer for the desired amount of time. Look into your partner's eyes.*

3. *Relax into your body, breathe deeply, and allow yourself to blink naturally. Keep your gaze soft and try not to look away.*

4. *Shift your gaze away from your partner when the timer goes off.*

The purpose of the exercise is to connect with your partner without speaking. If eye gazing feels uncomfortable at first, start with a shorter duration. Practice eye gazing for thirty seconds, then increase it gradually, working up to ten to twenty minutes.

Eye gazing face-to-face can be a little intense. It may be most appropriate for sparking romantic feelings. However, there are some variations of eye gazing that might work better for bonding and building trust in non-sexual relationships. Using a mirror to gaze at your partner can diffuse some of the intensity and still foster a deep connection.

You can build trust and offer and receive support using a mirror. Position a chair in front of a large mirror. The person receiving support sits in the chair facing the mirror. The person offering support stands behind them, looking into the mirror to make eye contact with the person seated. This exercise can be a compelling experience: a visual representation of one person supporting another, having their back if you will. It is a nice way to show your support to another without words. The person standing can put their hand on the other's shoulder, if that feels comfortable.

Vinai used this technique in the research on self-mirroring discussed in part 5. The therapist stands behind the client as they work through an issue.

You can also try eye gazing with two chairs side by side in front of a mirror. I discovered this when I got into a dispute with a good friend who is also a very creative person. We happened to be in an empty yoga studio at the time. So, we positioned two folding chairs side by side in front of the large studio mirror. We sat side by side, making eye contact and talking through the issue, holding hands. It was so powerful and effective: I understood her point of view and the emotions she had in a way that would not be possible if we tried to work it out face-to-face. When we are working on a creative project together, we'll occasionally do this just for fun. If we get stuck on a problem, one of us will invariably say, "Hey, let's go look in the mirror!" Mirror gazing side by side quite literally shifts our points of view.

In disputes, our perception can narrow to one person being right, one person being wrong, or one person is the good one, and one person is the bad one. When you are looking at both you and another, it's much harder to use black-and-white or polarizing thinking because you literally see your own and the other person's point of view. It can also diffuse any strong emotions like anger that could intensify through direct eye contact and get in the way of a productive conversation. When you can see yourself as you are talking with another, it's a total game-changer.

"Looking through the Eyes of Love" is a song by Melissa Manchester, and it's also a great strategy!

62. See Compassionately and Take Action

Once I was riding my bike down a steep hill and my tire got caught in a sewer grate. I catapulted over the handlebars and landed with such force that it knocked the wind out of me. Time stood still as I panicked, gasping for air. Eventually, I caught my breath and looked up to see I'd landed at the feet of a group of people in business suits waiting for the bus. They were all looking very uncomfortable, averting their gazes. None of them offered to help me or even ask if I was okay. They didn't seem to be intentionally hostile or unkind. Some pretended not to notice me, and others seemed unable to move as if frozen in fear. But clearly, there was no danger to them to offer me a hand. What happened? Why didn't they help?

Social psychologists have explained this tendency of groups to not offer help to a person in need as the bystander effect. People basically stand around wondering what to do and notice no one is doing anything, so they follow the norm. Individuals may also feel a diffusion of responsibility as in thinking, *Why should I help when there are so many other people here who can help?* This explains the phenomenon from an observer's perspective. But what's happening inside an individual witnessing someone in distress who doesn't make a move to help when there is no danger and minimal cost?

There are a variety of obstacles that can prevent us from putting our compassion into action. Why is it so difficult to show others that we care? How can we respond in ways that feel safe to ourselves and also benefit others?

Now that you have some techniques to see others with more compassion, let's consider how to put it into practice. As we learned, one of the quickest ways to avoid feeling anxious or threatened is to flee. By looking away from suffering, we may be visually fleeing from a person or situation which we see as threatening or overwhelming.

Neuroscience research can help us understand why empathy for others might not always let us take action.[64] Our ability to respond compassionately can be disrupted by our own reactions to seeing another person's distress. Yet, some people are extraordinarily good at helping others in distress. So how do they do it? Let's break it down into three steps.

Step 1. Recognize distress and feel emotional resonance.

If you can't recognize or feel another's distress, you obviously won't be moved to help them. We typically become aware of another person's distress by orienting toward their face. Seeing the look of distress on their face can automatically evoke the same feelings in us. So you may attempt to avoid this discomfort by simply looking away or distracting yourself. You may dodge looking directly at a suffering person, especially at their face or into their eyes, which convey the most emotion. To just look away or avoid seeing whatever is causing you discomfort is a very common and simple way to control your own emotions. You may also be more prone to avoid the suffering of others when you're already feeling stressed and anxious in the moment.

Step 2. Differentiate what's yours and what's theirs.

If you keep your attention on a distressed person, you can start to feel distressed yourself, which can be very uncomfortable, and for some people, it may even be confusing. If we are flooded with feelings of distress ourselves, it can be challenging to take action to help another person. Once you engage with a person suffering enough to feel empathy or emotional resonance, it may trigger your own trauma or a sense of helplessness, and you may go into the fight-flee-freeze stress response, being unable or unwilling to move toward the suffering or to help alleviate it. In this way, you can get stuck not being able to differentiate your own feelings from those you're witnessing in others.

Step 3. Act to alleviate distress and suffering.

So, to act compassionately, you must be able to handle your own negative emotions and not go into the fight-flee-freeze response. Neuroscience researchers have found that some people can better regulate their emotions and respond compassionately under stress, while others get stuck in their own reactions and can't seem to offer much help. *This difference is based on how their body responds to stress—not their attitudes toward people who are suffering.*

In this research, better self-regulation is measured by greater activity of the vagal nerve, which is the body's system to calm itself. Increases in vagal activity slow the heart and produce calm states that encourage social engagement and bonding with others. In addition, greater vagal activity indicates the ability to down-regulate negative emotions like distress so you can make more accurate appraisals when witnessing distress in others and decide what action to take to help them.

So, when some people seem to just naturally act more compassionately, it may be because they have better self-regulation, can manage their own distress, and then turn their attention to others. But anyone can learn to respond more compassionately. Having compassion for your own distress has been found to strengthen your ability to refocus and consciously activate self-regulation systems that create feelings of safety instead of feelings of threat and distress. These self-soothing activities operate by stimulating particular types of positive emotions, like contentment, security, and lovability, associated with our innate motivations for caring and attachment. In mirror meditation, particularly the exercises in part 5, you practice self-soothing, emotion regulation, and self-compassion. That'll help you to respond more compassionately to others too.

63. Reclaiming Your Projections

You can find numerous articles online about how to tell if someone is projecting onto you. But here, I'd like to suggest that you simply assume that others are projecting onto you all the time and that you are projecting onto them all the time too. Since you have little control over others and much more control over yourself, let's focus on increasing your awareness of how you might be projecting onto others. We will do this from a self-compassionate perspective. First, what is psychological projection?

Projection is basically not looking at yourself but looking at others and finding fault in them. Psychological projection is a defense mechanism people subconsciously employ to cope with difficult urges, feelings, or emotions. It involves projecting undesirable feelings or emotions onto someone else, rather than admitting to or dealing with the unwanted feelings yourself.

Mirror meditation may generally reduce projections because you are looking at yourself directly instead of seeing the flaws of others. You may be familiar with the quote attributed to Jesus that I'll paraphrase as, "Why look at the speck of sawdust in your neighbor's eye when you have a plank in your own eye?" Of course, it may be hard for you to imagine a plank in anyone's eye, especially your own, but I think you get the point.

Some psychologists have suggested that trying to suppress a thought actually gives it more power.[65] The unacceptable thought is constantly in your mental background and so significantly impacts how you see the world. Here are some examples of projection.

A woman who fears her partner will abandon her despite his reassurances. But she may be the one who wants to leave him, and that would be too disturbing to admit to herself.

A man in a committed relationship is attracted to a coworker, but rather than admit it to himself, he might accuse them of flirting with him.

If someone is wrestling with the urge to steal something, they might come to believe their neighbors are trying to break into their home.

We tend to project when something about ourselves is too difficult to acknowledge. Rather than confronting it, we cast it onto someone else. This way, we can keep our anxiety in check, make difficult emotions more tolerable, and avoid the difficult emotions and self-judgments resulting from owning it. Sometimes it's easier to attack or witness wrongdoing in another person than confront that possibility in your own behavior. How a person acts toward the target of their projection might reflect how they feel about themselves.

Ironically, when projection is working well, you won't even realize that you're doing it. Projection occurs unconsciously, but these patterns can be brought to conscious awareness, especially with the help of a therapist. When your fears or insecurities are provoked, it's natural to project onto others. Here is an exercise that you can try on your own with your self-reflection tools.

- - - **try this** - - -

If you think you might be projecting, your first move should be to step away from any conflict. Time away will allow your defensiveness to fade a bit so you can consider the situation more objectively. Then make a video journal using the third-person perspective and do these three steps in order.

1. Describe the conflict in objective terms.

2. Describe the actions you took and the assumption you made.

3. Describe the action the other person took and the assumption they made.

Watch the video from a centered, calm perspective. Then, consider watching it with your therapist or a trusted friend to get their point of view too.

64. When Others Look Threatening

After a messy divorce, Frank moved to a new condo, eager for a fresh start. The first morning he was woken at 5:00 a.m. to the sound of breaking glass. As he lay in bed, he heard the breaking over and over again. The sound seemed to be coming from outside his balcony. He opened the door and walked outside. The culprit: wind chimes!! Frank immediately blew, "What the F---!" How could everybody be so stupid and inconsiderate to hang wind chimes right above his balcony? Then he started to wonder: His new upstairs neighbors were polite but not too friendly. Maybe there were just seeing what they could get away with? Perhaps they were trying to test him? Or were they making fun of him? Or they wanted to assert dominance over him because they, after all, lived above him? Maybe they felt superior to him because they lived above him, and they were just trying to rub it in?

In reality, Frank's neighbors were pretty peaceful people; they enjoyed the wind chimes, which sounded to them like gentle tinkling music in the breeze. They did not think anyone else could even hear them, let alone be bothered by them. But Frank was off to the races with his egregious story.

Frank has a type-A personality. Type-A personalities generally feel a sense of limited time, urgency, and competitiveness; they also tend to display a good deal of hostility. Hostility is strongly linked to heart disease as well as interpersonal difficulties. When you have free-floating hostility, you are much more likely to attribute hostile intent to others. Psychologists have identified hostile intent attribution (HIA) as an actual thing: the tendency to attribute hostile intent to others in social situations with a negative outcome for the individual. The other person's intention is ambiguous. HIA is a special kind of projection that is surprisingly common. You may have seen it online, in-person, or on the road, among other places.

We tend to conflate impact with intention. That is, if someone does something that creates a huge negative impact on you, you're likely to think they did it on purpose. When we assume that someone was intentionally trying to harm us, the conflict often escalates. The key is to separate your reaction from what objectively happened and then find the solution. Also, it's important not to take anything personally. Frank's neighbors did not intend to wake him up at 5:00 a.m. or send him a message about his standing in the community.

Frank followed the steps to work with projection described in the last chapter. He stepped away from the conflict. He described it objectively: neighbor's wind chimes are disrupting his sleep. Frank looked at his assumptions through the third-person perspective.

When he watched the video, the shift in perspective helped him realize his assumptions were probably not accurate. His messy divorce and various gossip led him to lose status in his former community. He carried that concern as he moved to a new community. He grew up in a very competitive family with many brothers and sisters who were constantly vying for their parents' attention and trying to outdo each other in sports and at school. They now kept score by acquiring status symbols, like an attractive partner, material wealth, important job titles, and the like. After his divorce, Frank was extra sensitive about his status. Consciously, he thought it was silly to worry what people thought. It was hard for him to see how much he wanted to be respected and liked by his new neighbors. Projection allowed him to suppress his feelings of inferiority and vulnerability.

Once he realized that, I suggested he do some role-playing in the mirror. Frank was able to shift out of seeing the situation through the lens of hostility. Instead, he imagined his neighbors were reasonable people and focused on his desire to be respected and have good communication. Through role-playing in the mirror, Frank was able to see the situation more objectively. Then by practicing the conversation with his neighbors ahead of time, he could have a much more productive discussion with them.

65. Out of the Shadow: Facing Contempt

A few years ago, I was in an unpleasant roommate situation. One day I was making a video journal in my bedroom when my roommate yelled a request at me through the door. My face momentarily contorted into an ugly expression I'd never seen before. As I watched the video, it looked like a mixture of annoyance, disgust, and exasperation. This was very curious. I did a bit of research and found out it was *contempt!* I did not think I showed contempt for anyone, but apparently, I did, as it is a human emotion, and I am human. And I caught it on video.

Contempt is a shadow emotion for many people like me. I did not grow up talking about contempt around the dinner table, at least not directly. The dictionary says contempt is a pattern of attitudes and behavior, often toward an individual or group, but sometimes toward an ideology, which has the characteristics of disgust and anger. The word becomes from the Latin word for scorn.

Contempt is classified as one of the seven basic emotions. We can think of contempt on the same continuum as resentment and anger, but the differences between the three are that resentment is often anger directed toward a higher-status individual; anger is directed toward an equal-status individual, and contempt is anger directed toward a lower-status individual.

Treating someone with contempt means that you treat someone as though they are beneath you, not worthy of your consideration or kindness. When we treat people with contempt, it is a sign that we are not seeing them as a person. We see them as something below us, and we despise them. You may feel people are underneath you if they hold different opinions on politics, dietary preferences, religion, you name it. We tend to believe we are the most informed person in any debate, so if others don't agree with us, they are ignorant and therefore beneath us.

Of course, no one likes being treated with contempt, and it can become very difficult to change someone's mind when they sense you regard them with contempt. For instance, Rita dreaded going back home for the holidays because her family had strong political beliefs that she vehemently disagreed with. In fact, Rita had a PhD in political science, so she knew she was clearly the most well-informed and an expert on the issues. Yet, her high-school-educated family thought she was simply being arrogant—they sensed her contempt for them—and went out of their way to return it in kind.

As a mirror meditation student, Rita thought she was struggling with anger, but it was really contempt. She tended to feel superior to others to compensate for her humble beginnings.

I suggested she do some role-playing research in the mirror. She could bring to mind one of her relatives who triggered her and imagine having a conversation with them. In her role-playing, she saw what I saw in my bedroom that day with my roommate yelling at me: contempt.

She watched the one side of her mouth tighten as her face morphed into contempt. Most facial expressions look the same on both sides of the face, but contempt happens on only one side. The expression of contempt can occur with a hint of a smile, as if to say, "I'm enjoying seeing how inferior you are." Or it can be part of an angry expression, as in "You're so stupid you don't even know it!" Contempt can also show up as a mean-girl smirk. Research shows that girls are more likely to display nonverbal forms of social aggression, like speaking sweetly with a contemptuous look.[66] Contempt can run the gamut from a bit playful to deadly serious.

I suggested Rita spend some time getting to know her contemptuous side. So she could own it and accept it as part of herself. In her research, she experimented with role-playing from the first, second, and third perspectives in her video journal:

I feel contempt for X.

You feel contempt by X.

Rita feels contempt because...

X is (disgusting....)

Contempt is often a shadow emotion, in that we might not be aware that we are expressing it. When we feel people are beneath us, for whatever reason, we think our view is justified, so we tend not to question it. But contempt can create stubborn divisions between people that make difficulties quite challenging to resolve. There has been a good deal of research on the role of contempt in the dissolutions of committed relationships. According to renowned relationship researcher John Gottman, contemptuous behavior like eye-rolling, sarcasm, and name-calling is the number one predictor of divorce.

Feeling contempt on occasion is part of being human, but there's no reason to get stuck there. Instead, you can bring your feelings to light, take a good look, and change your perspective to see others more compassionately, and realistically too.

- - - try this - - -

You can work to increase your awareness of how you may be inadvertently expressing contempt with your video journal. There are three stages to this process.

Stage 1: Venting. This is exactly what it sounds like. First, allow yourself to say whatever you want to say about the person you feel contempt toward (or someone you feel superior to and can't stand). Then watch your videos from a calm, centered space.

Stage 2: Awareness. In this stage, you describe the person and your issues with them from a third-person perspective. Then watch the video from a calm, centered space.

Stage 3: Reparation. Make a video role-playing the other person. Imagine them watching the videos of you describing them in a contemptuous fashion and share your reactions from their perspective.

This exercise has been amazingly powerful for my students and me. However, it is vital that you do this with self-compassion and the intention of increasing your self-awareness. You may decide not to even bring the issue up with the other person, but your view of them is guaranteed to change!

Resentment is the reverse of contempt. It occurs when you feel angry, inferior, and powerless, like anger with your boss or someone you feel has power over you. You can do the same set of self-reflection exercises to shift out of resentment too.

66. The Beauty Bias: Idolizing Others

Not all our biases are negative. But even positive ones can be just as inaccurate and prevent you from making an authentic connection. For instance, Ruby idolized Bruce even though her friends, and even Bruce himself, tried to tell her he was not really the way she imagined he was. Bruce looked like he walked off the cover of *GQ* magazine. Ruby fell in love with him at first sight. Any man that handsome must be divine, magical, talented, kind, and brilliant, she thought. But in reality, Bruce was different. He was not particularly interested in sex, especially not with Ruby. Aside from his looks, he was an average guy, with modest career goals, and as an introvert who spent much of his free time playing video games, he found parties and social functions tedious.

The "beauty bias" operates in almost all social situations. Research shows that we react more favorably to physically attractive people.[67] We believe in the "what is beautiful is good" stereotype, an irrational but deep-seated belief that physically attractive people possess other desirable characteristics such as intelligence, competence, social skills, confidence, and even moral virtue. Beautiful people have distinct advantages in our society. Studies show attractive children are more popular, both with classmates and teachers. Teachers give higher evaluations to the work of attractive children and have higher expectations (which has been shown to improve performance).[68] Attractive applicants have a better chance of getting jobs and of receiving higher salaries.[69] In court, beautiful people are found guilty less often.[70] When found guilty, they receive less severe sentences. Yet, studies show that attractive people don't benefit from the "beauty bias" in terms of self-esteem.[71] They often don't trust praise of their work or talents and seem to know that their appearance influences positive evaluations.

Ruby found it hard to accept that Bruce was not interested in her. Bruce had met women like Ruby before. He was willing to chat politely, but he had no desire to pursue a relationship with them, mainly because he sensed they had already made their minds about him without even knowing him. Ruby eventually confronted Bruce and asked him if he was gay. Being gay was the only reason she could think of for why he did not want to go out with her. Bruce refused to answer the question. His sexuality was his own business, and just because many women (and men) found him attractive did not mean he owed them an explanation about his preferences. Bruce actually preferred not to date anyone who seemed to fall for him at first sight because he knew it would lead to mutual disappointment. Instead, he liked to take his time to get to know someone as a friend before anything else happened.

In contrast, Paul was a self-proclaimed playboy. He dated many beautiful women. His friends referred to them as "the flavor of the month." Paul flaunted his glamourous girlfriends on the surface, but deep down, he was troubled that he couldn't find a relationship that would stick. It seemed that every woman Paul ever dated turned out to be a liar who betrayed him. How did this happen?

Well, many of these girlfriends took The Man Magnet or similar courses on how to seduce men by looking sexy, acting sexy, and engaging in flirtatious, seductive conversations. Paul loved it. But he noticed that all his beautiful girlfriends would eventually change. They did not want to get up and do a fifty-minute hair and makeup routine, put on form-fitted undergarments and a body-con dress, go to the kitchen, and cook Paul's breakfast with a pleasing smile. They wanted to lie in bed with sleep in their eyes; they yawned and farted and sometimes had bad breath. Some liked to pad around his apartment in sweatpants and an old sports bra; they laughed and made crude jokes with their women friends on the phone.

What happened to Paul's gorgeous girlfriends? Each girlfriend was unique in her defiance of Paul's expectations. But in every case, he concluded that she had just been putting on an act because she wanted his money. Once she revealed her true self as a "gold digger," Paul yelled, "Next!" Paul seemed to ignore the fact that he stayed bed in with sleep in his eyes; he yawned, belched, farted, and shuffled around in his underwear yelling on the phone too. Somehow that was okay for him, but because his girlfriends were so physically beautiful, he expected them to be unwaveringly beautiful in every little thing they did. No woman could or would put up with his unrealistic expectations.

Both Ruby and Paul could benefit from doing the "Are you?" exercise introduced at the beginning of this section. Role-playing in the mirror could also take them deeper into their true needs for a partner. Maybe they were projecting some of their unowned positive qualities onto their love interests instead of seeing these qualities in themselves?

- - - try this - - -

Next time you have a crush on someone that seems like it might be a bit unrealistic, try these steps in your video journal. Make a video journal using the third-person perspective and do the three steps in order. For example, "Tara is very attracted to person X."

1. Describe what it is about the person that you find attractive in objective terms.

2. Describe the actions you took and the assumptions you made based on these characteristics.

3. Describe the action the other person took and the assumptions they made.

Watch the video from a centered, calm perspective. Then, consider watching it with your therapist or a trusted friend to get their point of view too.

Conclusion:
Living Reflectively

Mirror meditation may conjure images of a beautiful goddess with long glossy locks, batting thick eyelashes, as she gazes hypnotically at herself, dabbing aromatic oil on her décolletage, but maybe she's feeling like a phony? She can also be walking down street on a windy day and turning her video camera on herself, plucking stray hairs out of her lip gloss with mascara flakes under her eyes, looking a bit tired and puffy, and being totally okay with it! Realizing you don't have to be perfect to look at yourself or to be seen by others is the cardinal benefit of mirror meditation. And, checking in to see how you're feeling should now be your priority.

Have you ever noticed that couples who've been happily together for a long time seem to have a set of shared stories? Remembering these experiences helps build appreciation, affection, and cohesion in their relationship. Having someone around who loves you and who'll remind you of your goodness greatly benefits our well-being. We often rely on others close to us to tell us the stories of the good stuff; the positive memories that give us a sense of comfort, belonging, and efficacy.

You now have the tools to enjoy a caring and supportive relationship with yourself always —regardless of your life circumstances.

If you do mirror meditation and video journaling regularly, you'll discover that it provides a sense of continuity over time. In doing my mirror meditation and video journals for over ten years, I've experienced so many life changes. I was constantly glad to have my mirror meditation and video journaling practices to turn to regularly. No matter what was happening in my life, there I was, consistently looking at myself in the mirror, for better or worse! It gave me a sense of comfort and predictability, despite all the changes. It helped me adjust to the changes in my relationships with others while it strengthened my relationship with myself. It's such a cliché to say your longest relationship is with yourself! But everyone discovers that for themselves, eventually. So make your relationship with yourself a kind one, a strong one—and a consistent one —with video journaling. Sounds like an ad. I know. But it's true.

My students have discovered many benefits from self-reflection with mirror mediation and video journaling. These benefits seem to increase with time. After you've been doing these self-reflection practices for a while, you may find it striking to see how much you've have grown and to see the many life challenges you have navigated successfully. Here is a list of the most common benefits you'll discover from meditating with a mirror and video journaling regularly.

1. Illuminate Your Ability to Solve Problems

As discussed earlier, we have a strong negativity bias, so adverse events stand out much more prominently in our minds than positive ones. It's as if our mind says, "That worked out, so I can forget about it." We can easily forget all the challenges we've successfully handled and how much we're growing as a result. In addition to the negativity bias, we also tend to remember uncompleted or interrupted tasks better than completed ones—this is called the "Zeigarnik effect." So when you review your video journal, you'll be amazed at the number of activities, problems, and tasks you completed successfully that you simply forgot. Seeing it in your video journal can give you a boost in confidence and help you remember just how competent you are.

2. Provide Perspective

When you allow your mind to wander aloud in your video journal, it'll naturally gravitate toward anything that you're worried about. In reviewing your videos, you'll gain a powerful perspective on just how much your worrying affects you. You may also realize how small and inconsequential many of these issues are. For instance, Lisa worked at a part-time job and struggled to deal with her boss's critical comments. When she reviewed her videos, she saw how much time she spent time going over what her boss said to her. She realized she took a lot of what her boss said to heart, and she was upsetting herself by replaying the comments repeatedly in her mind when she did her mirror meditation and her video journal. Later, after she left the job, she looked back on her videos and realized how much time she wasted in this stressful experience, worrying what someone she'd probably never see again thought of her. To help put worries in perspective, therapists and coaches often advise people to consider how significant a particular problem will be a year from now. In the mirror and your videos, you'll see for yourself!

3. Validate Your Intuition and Hunches

As you face yourself in the mirror and use your video journal to discuss your *uncensored* thoughts and feelings about people and situations, you'll see the usefulness of your hunches. Often, we can be in the habit of censoring ourselves. A small voice inside might say, "That person is creepy," then it quickly gets overridden by more pleasant thoughts. We can also perceive people as having negative qualities because they remind us of someone from our past—when the person really doesn't have this quality at all. With video journaling, you can test out your hunches. When you have a slight twinge of suspicion about someone and you share it in your video journal, you can look back six months down the road after you've entered into a romantic relationship or business contract with them. Was your intuition correct? What about the times when you had a bad feeling about something and nothing bad happened? If you share these hunches in your video and look back on them, you'll learn a lot about your patterns of sizing people and situations up, and you'll get better at it. You'll learn to trust yourself more.

4. Build a Vault of Creative Ideas

Giving yourself ten minutes a day to say anything you want can be daunting—and incredibly liberating. My students report many creative ideas, projects, and solutions from just letting themselves talk and wondering about anything they want without the pressure of having to "be creative." Some also get in the habit of whipping out their video camera to make a short video whenever they get a creative spark. They capture the idea and their enthusiasm about the idea before any critical voices—internal or external—can get their hands on it! It's also fun to look back on some of your crazier ideas over time; it can give you a good laugh.

5. Foster Gratitude

One of the most potent experiences students have in looking back on their videos is witnessing what they were like *before* something life-changing happened. Seeing yourself wanting what you now have can give you a new perspective on your life. Students often report a natural upwelling of gratitude. They also appreciate their struggle and their ability to persevere through challenges to achieve their goals. They savor the experiences now past, such as looking back on sharing experiences from a day with a loved one who's no longer living. These kinds of experiences are precious and typically lost in our memory.

Thank you for going on this journey of self-discovery with me. I hope you'll continue to reach for your mirror and video journal regularly. You'll find that there is much more to discover as you continue to build an honest, caring, compassionate relationship with yourself.

When you pass by a mirror, I hope you'll always remember to see your own image as a source of comfort, appreciation, and pleasure. I hope that seeing yourself continues to remind you just how magnificent you are!

Acknowledgments

Looking at yourself in the mirror is not always easy. Thank you to all those who had the willingness to do it and share their experiences with me. Without your honesty and courage, this book could not have been written.

If everyone congratulated me on my brilliance in developing the concept of mirror meditation, this book would have been pretty vacuous. So, I appreciate my critics who took the time to voice their concerns and skepticism—subtly and vigorously, large and small—on the idea of mirror meditation. Those critiques helped me to write a more compassionate book.

Thanks to the team at New Harbinger: Jennye Garibaldi, Jennifer Holder, and Wendy Millstone for your enthusiasm and helpful feedback on this book. Thanks to Amy Shoup for a fantastic cover design and Gretel Hakanson for her careful edits.

Special thanks to my agent Mel Parker who was willing to take a chance and guide me through the publication waters. His support has been stellar.

Many thanks to the members of the Barnard community. I greatly appreciate the support from Deborah Spar, Sian Beilock, and Linda Bell. Thanks to my colleagues who gave me wise writing advice: Jennifer Finney Boylan, Tovah Klein, Scott Barry Kaufman, and Alexandra Horowitz. Special thanks to Peter Balsam for his unflagging goodwill throughout the years.

Thanks to Ann Alexander, Tasha Eurich, Mark Epstein, Kristin Neff, Melanie Greenberg, Valerie Monroe, Margie Warrell, Barbara Stanny-Huson, Juna Bobby, Yvette LeBlowitz, Betsy Rapoport, Linda Sivertsen, and Charlotte Lieberman for their interest and support for this project.

Thanks to the Society for Personology. Dan McAdams, Jefferson Singer, Ed de St. Aubin, and Jack Bauer offered insightful suggestions when I was at the very beginning of the process of thinking about mirrors and emotion—thanks for your openness and patience.

Special thanks to Tim McHenry and The Rubin Museum of Art for sponsoring the public debut of Mirror Meditation. This was a delightful and magical experience that I will never forget.

Many thanks to Manal Fakhoury, Rena Romano, Trisha Brouk, and all those who helped make TEDx Ocala 2019: Reflection a great success. This was a wonderful moment that opened the door for many great possibilities.

Thanks to the many students who devoted their enthusiasm and hard work to the mirror meditation research project. Special thanks to Jessica Gunther, Lisa Levenson, Breena Moore, Quadrina Noori, Princess Jael, Sophia Quraishi, Alaira Shetty, Maria Tomilenko, and Josie Zena-Fazzino.

This book weaves together many different learning experiences and threads of wisdom offered by countless great teachers I have had the privilege to know and learn from. Sincere thanks to Mary Abrams, Elizabeth Andes-Bell, Joel Aronoff, Bruce Bell, Barbara Brennan, Mary Ann Bruning, Julia Cameron, Diana Muenz Chen, Deepak Chopra, Emile Conrad, David Ellzey, Joan Halifax, Susan Harper, David Lobenstine, Joyce Lunsford-Crum, Piper Makepeace, Michael Mervosh, Suzi Tucker, Kasia Urbaniak, and John Kabat-Zinn.

Thank you to my life-long friends who have supported me and this project in big and small ways: Marilyn, Karen, Kate, Barbara, Lorraine, Sparky, David, and Stuart. I value our friendship.

Endnotes

1 Kjerstin Gruys, *Mirror, Mirror Off the Wall* (New York: Penguin, 2014); Lara Parker, "This Is What Happened When I Didn't Look in The Mirror for a Week," *Buzz Feed*, May 28, 2015.

2 Yumiko Otsuka, "Face Recognition in Infants: A Review of Behavioral and Near-Infrared Spectroscopic Studies," *Japanese Psychological Research* 56, no. 1 (January 2014): 76–90.

3 Philippe Rochat, Tanya Broesch, and Katherin Jayne, "Social Awareness and Early Self-Recognition," *Consciousness and Cognition* 21, no. 3 (September 2012): 1491–1497.

4 Catherine Bortolon and Stephanie Raffard, "Self-Face Advantage over Familiar and Unfamiliar Faces: A Three-Level Meta-Analytic Approach," *Psychonomic Bulletin Review* 25, no. 4 (2018): 1287–1300.

5 Chisa Ota and Tamani Nakano, "Self-Face Activates the Dopamine Reward Pathway Without Awareness," *Cerebral Cortex* (April 16, 2021).

6 Andrea Zaccaro, et al., "How Breath-Control Can Change Your Life: A Systematic Review on Psycho-Physiological Correlates of Slow Breathing," *Frontiers in Human Neuroscience* 12 (September 7, 2018): 353.

7 Laura Herrador Colmenero, et al., "Effectiveness of Mirror Therapy, Motor Imagery, and Virtual Feedback on Phantom Limb Pain Following Amputation," *Prosthetics and Orthotics International* 42, no. 3 (June 2018): 288–298.

8 David A. Frederick, Gaganjyot Sandhu, Patrick J. Morse, and Viren Swami, "Correlates of Appearance and Weight Satisfaction in a US National Sample: Personality, Attachment Style, Television Viewing, Self-Esteem, and Life Satisfaction," *Body Image* 17 (2016): 191–203.

9   John Cacioppo, Stephanie Cacioppo, and Jackie Gollan, "The Negativity Bias: Conceptualization, Quantification, and Individual Differences," *Behavioral and Brain Sciences* 37, no. 3 (March 2014): 309–310.

10 Kate Fox, "Mirror, Mirror: A Summary of Research Findings on Body Image," *Social Issues Research Centre* (1997).

11 Rachel Calogero, *Self-Objectification in Women: Causes, Consequences, and Counteractions* (Washington, DC: American Psychological Association, 2011).

12 Juliana G. Breines, Jennifer Crocker, and Julie A. Garcia, "Self-Objectification and Well-Being in Women's Daily Lives," *Personality and Social Psychology Bulletin* 34, no. 5 (May 2008): 583–598.

13 Rotem Kahalon, Nurit Shnabel, and Julia Becker, "Experimental Studies on State Self-Objectification: A Review and an Integrative Process Model," *Frontiers in Psychology* 9 (August 13, 2018): 1268.

14 Barbara Fredrickson, et al., "That Swimsuit Becomes You: Sex Differences in Self-Objectification, Restrained Eating, and Math Performance," *Journal of Personality and Social Psychology* 75, no. 1 (July 1998): 269–284.

15 Rachel Calogero, "Objects Don't Object: Evidence That Self-Objectification Disrupts Women's Social Activism," *Psychological Science* 24, no. 3 (March 2013): 312–318.

16 Anton Minty and Gavin Minty, "The Prevalence of Body Dysmorphic Disorder in the Community: A Systematic Review," *Global Psychiatry* (2021): 130–154.

17 Francesca Beilharz, David Castle, Sally Grace, and Susan Rossell, "A Systematic Review of Visual Processing and Associated Treatments in Body Dysmorphic Disorder," *Acta Psychiatrica Scandinavica* 136, no. 1 (July 2017): 16–36.

18 Wei Lin Toh, David Castle, and Susan Rossell, "How Individuals with Body Dysmorphic Disorder (BDD) Process Their Own Face: A Quantitative and Qualitative Investigation Based on an Eye-Tracking Paradigm," *Cognitive Neuropsychiatry* 22, no. 3 (May 2017): 213–232.

19 Trevor Griffen, Eva Naumann, and Tom Hildebrandt, "Mirror Exposure Therapy for Body Image Disturbances and Eating Disorders: A Review," *Clinical Psychology Review* 65 (November 2018): 163–174.

20 Fox, "Mirror, Mirror."

21 Alexander James Kirkham, Julian Michael Breeze, and Paloma Marí-Beffa, "The Impact of Verbal Instructions on Goal-Directed Behaviour," *Acta Psychologica* 139, no. 1 (January 2012): 212–219.

22 Gary Lupyan and Daniel Swingley, "Self-Directed Speech Affects Visual Search Performance," *Quarterly Journal of Experimental Psychology* 65, no. 6 (June 2012): 1068–1085.

23 Holly E. Brophy-Herb, et al., "Terrific Twos: Promoting Toddlers' Competencies in the Context of Important Relationships," in *Building Early Social and Emotional Relationships with Infants and Toddlers,* eds. A. Morris and A. Williamson (Cham, Switzerland: Springer Nature, 2018).

24 Antonis Hatzigeorgiadis, Nikos Zourbanos, Evangelos Galanis, and Yiannis Theodorakis, "Self-Talk and Sports Performance: A Meta-Analysis," *Perspectives on Psychological Science* 6, no. 4 (July 2011): 348–356.

25 Ethan Kross, et al., "Self-Talk as a Regulatory Mechanism: How You Do It Matters," *Journal of Personality and Social Psychology* 106, no. 2 (February 2014): 304–324.

26 Jason Moser, et al., "Third-Person Self-Talk Facilitates Emotion Regulation Without Engaging Cognitive Control: Converging Evidence from ERP and fMRI," *Scientific Reports* 7 (July 2017): 4519.

27 Kristin Neff, "Self-Compassion: An Alternative Conceptualization of a Healthy Attitude Toward Oneself," *Self and Identity* 2, no. 2: 85–101.

28 Jennifer Stellar, Adam Cohen, Christopher Oveis, and Dacher Keltner, "Affective and Physiological Responses to the Suffering of Others: Compassion and Vagal Activity," Journal of Personality and Social Psychology 108, no. 4 (April 2015): 572–585.

29 Nicola Petrocchi, Cristina Ottaviani, and Alessandro Couyoumdjian, "Compassion at the Mirror: Exposure to a Mirror Increases the Efficacy of a Self-Compassion Manipulation in Enhancing Soothing Positive Affect and Heart Rate Variability," *The Journal of Positive Psychology* 12, no. 6 (June 2017): 525–536.

30 James Pennebaker, "Expressive Writing in Psychological Science," *Perspectives on Psychological Science* 13, no. 2 (March 2018): 226–229.

31 Nielsen, "Time Flies: US Adults Now Spend Nearly Half a Day Interacting with Media," July 31, 2018.

32 Betul Keles, Niall McCrae, and Annmarie Grealish, "A Systematic Review: The Influence of Social Media on Depression, Anxiety and Psychological Distress in Adolescents," *International Joukrnal of Adolescence and Youth* 25, no. 1 (January 2020): 79–93.

33 Christopher T. Barry, et al., "'Check Your Selfie Before You Wreck Your Selfie': Personality Ratings of Instagram Users as a Function of Self-Image Posts," *Journal of Research in Personality* 82 (2019): 103843.

34 Janarthanan Balakrishnan and Mark D. Griffiths, "An Exploratory Study of 'Selfitis' and the Development of the Selfitis Behavior Scale," *International Journal of Mental Health and Addiction* 16 (March 2018): 722–736.

35 Ayelet Meron Ruscio, et al., "Cross-Sectional Comparison of the Epidemiology of *DSM-5* Generalized Anxiety Disorder Across the Globe," *JAMA Psychiatry* 74, no. 5 (2017): 465–475.

36 Piergiuseppe Vinai, et al., "The Clinical Implications and Neurophysiological Background of Using Self-Mirroring Technique to Enhance the Identification of Emotional Experiences: An Example with Rational Emotive Behavior Therapy," *Journal of Rational-Emotive Cognitive-Behavioral Therapy* 33 (2015): 115–133.

37 Nielsen, "Time Flies."

38 Holly Shakya and Nicholas Christakis, "Association of Facebook Use with Compromised Well-Being: A Longitudinal Study," *American Journal Epidemiology* 185, no. 3 (February 1, 2017): 203–211.

39 Mental Health America, "Number of People Reporting Anxiety and Depression Nationwide Since Start of Pandemic Hits All-Time High in September, Hitting Young People Hardest," October 20, 2020.

40 American Psychological Association, "Stress in America 2020: A National Mental Health Crisis," online report, 2020.

41 Dan Grupe and Jack Nitschke, "Uncertainty and Anticipation in Anxiety: An Integrated Neurobiological and Psychological Perspective," *Nature Reviews Neuroscience* 14, no. 7 (July 2013): 488–501.

42 Vinai et al., "Clinical Implications."

43 Bobby Azarian, "How Anxiety Warps Your Perception," *BBC Future,* September 26, 2016.

44 Judson Brewer, "A 10-Second Eye Exercise to Calm Your Mind," *Medium,* April 29, 2020.

45 David Orme-Johnson and Vernon Barnes, "Effects of the Transcendental Meditation Technique on Trait Anxiety: A Meta-Analysis of Randomized Controlled Trials," *Journal of Alternative and Complementary Medicine* 20, no. 5 (May 2014): 330–341.

46 Martin Wegrzyn, et al., "Mapping the Emotional Face. How Individual Face Parts Contribute to Successful Emotion Recognition," *PloS One* 12, no. 5 (May. 2017): e0177239.

47 Miho Iwasaki and Yasuki Noguchi, "Hiding True Emotions: Micro-Expressions in Eyes Retrospectively Concealed by Mouth Movements," *Science Reports* 6 (2016): 22049.

48 Ute Hülsheger and Anna Schewe, "On the Costs and Benefits of Emotional Labor: A Meta-Analysis of Three Decades of Research," *Journal of Occupational Health Psychology* 16, no. 3 (March 2011): 361–389.

49 Jun Zhan, Hongfei Xu, Jun Ren, and Jing Luo, "Is Catharsis Beneficial or Harmful? The Psychological Intervention Effect and Potential Harm of Catharsis," *Advances in Psychological Science* 28, no. 1 (January 2020): 22–32.

50 American Psychiatric Association. *Diagnostic and Statistical Manual of Mental Disorders,* 5th ed. (Arlington, VA: American Psychiatric Association, 2013).

51 Teresa Farroni, et al., "Eye Contact Detection in Humans from Birth," *Proceedings of the National Academy of Sciences of the United States of America* 99, no. 14 (2002): 9602–9605.

52 Tania Singer and Olga Klimecki, "Empathy and Compassion," *Current Biology* 24, no. 18 (September 22, 2014): 875–878.

53 Kamila Jankowiak-Siuda and Wojciech Zajkowski, "A Neural Model of Mechanisms of Empathy Deficits in Narcissism," *Medical Science Monitor: International Medical Journal of Experimental and Clinical Research* 19 (November 5, 2013), 934–941.

54 Marlies Marissen, Mathijs Deen, and Ingmar Franken, "Disturbed Emotion Recognition in Patients with Narcissistic Personality Disorder," *Psychiatry Research* 198, no. 2 (July 30, 2012): 269–273.

55 Nicholas Holtzman and Michael Strube, "Narcissism and Attractiveness," *Journal of Research in Personality* 44, no. 1 (2010): 133–136.

56 Bill Thornton and Jason Maurice, "Physical Attractiveness Contrast Effect and the Moderating Influence of Self-Consciousness," *Sex Roles* 40 (1999): 379–392.

57 Adam Lipson, David Przybyla, and Donn Byrne. "Physical Attractiveness, Self-Awareness, and Mirror-Gazing Behavior," *Bulletin of the Psychonomic Society* 21, no. 2 (February 1983): 115–116.

58 Christopher Masi, Hsi-Yuan Chen, Louise C. Hawkley, and John T. Cacioppo. "A Meta-Analysis of Interventions to Reduce Loneliness," *Personality and Social Psychology Review* 15, no. 3 (August 2011): 219–266.

59 Andy Arnold, "Smile (but Only Deliberately) Though Your Heart Is Aching: Loneliness Is Associated with Impaired Spontaneous Smile Mimicry," *PsyArXiv* (April 17, 2019).

60 D. W. Winnicott, "The Capacity to Be Alone," *International Journal of Psychoanalysis* 39: 416–420.

61 Jari Hietanen, "Affective Eye Contact: An Integrative Review," *Frontiers in Psychology* 9 (August 28, 2018): 1587.

62 New York Times, "Can You Read People's Emotions?" *The Well Quiz,* October 3, 2013.

63 Miho Nagasawa, et al., "Oxytocin-Gaze Positive Loop and the Coevolution of Human-Dog Bonds," *Science* 348 (April 17, 2015): 333–336.

64 Stellar et al., "Affective and Physiological Responses."

65 Leonard Newman, Kimberley Duff, and Roy Baumeister, "A New Look at Defensive Projection: Thought Suppression, Accessibility, and Biased Person Perception," *Journal of Personality and Social Psychology* 72, no. 5 (May 1997): 980–100.

66 Susan A. Basow, et al., "Perceptions of Relational and Physical Aggression Among College Students: Effects of Gender of Perpetrator, Target, and Perceiver," *Psychology of Women Quarterly* 31, no. 1 (2007): 85–95.

67 Sean Talamas, et al., "Blinded by Beauty: Attractiveness Bias and Accurate Perceptions of Academic Performance," *PloS One* 11, no. 2 (February 17, 2016): e0148284.

68 Margaret M. Clifford and Elaine Walster, "The Effect of Physical Attractiveness on Teacher Expectations," *Sociology of Education* 46, no. 2 (1973): 248–258.

69 Bradley Ruffle and Ze'ev Shtudiner, "Are Good-Looking People More Employable?" *Management Science* 61 (2011), https://doi.org/10.2139/ssrn.1705244.

70 Justin Gunnell and Stephen Ceci, "When Emotionality Trumps Reason: A Study of Individual Processing Styles and Juror Bias," *Behavioral Sciences and the Law* 28, no. 6 (November 25, 2010): 850–877.

71 Fox, "Mirror, Mirror."

Tara Well, PhD, is associate professor of psychology at Barnard College of Columbia University in New York, NY, where she developed a mirror-based meditation called "a revelation" in *The New York Times*. As an expert on self-awareness, body-image, self-compassion, emotional resilience, and meditation, Well has appeared on *NBC Nightly News* and has been quoted in *The New York Times, The Boston Globe, The Washington Post, Bloomberg, Vice, Forbes, Harper's Bazaar, Shape, Allure,* and other media publications. In 2019, she gave the TEDx Talk, "What Mirror Meditation Can Teach You." Her blog, *The Clarity on Psychology Today,* has more than a million readers. You can learn more about Well at www.mirrormeditation.com.

Real change *is* possible

For more than forty-five years, New Harbinger has published proven-effective self-help books and pioneering workbooks to help readers of all ages and backgrounds improve mental health and well-being, and achieve lasting personal growth. In addition, our spirituality books offer profound guidance for deepening awareness and cultivating healing, self-discovery, and fulfillment.

Founded by psychologist Matthew McKay and Patrick Fanning, New Harbinger is proud to be an independent, employee-owned company. Our books reflect our core values of integrity, innovation, commitment, sustainability, compassion, and trust. Written by leaders in the field and recommended by therapists worldwide, New Harbinger books are practical, accessible, and provide real tools for real change.

 **newharbinger**publications

MORE BOOKS from
NEW HARBINGER PUBLICATIONS

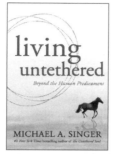
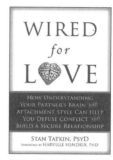
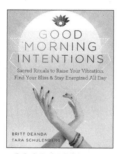

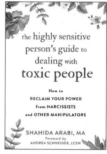